MANAGEMENT'S ROLE

in

LOSS PREVENTION

CHARLES F. HEMPHILL, Jr.

A DIVISION OF AMERICAN MANAGEMENT ASSOCIATIONS

Library of Congress Cataloging in Publication Data

Hemphill, Charles F
    Management's role in loss prevention.

    Includes index.
    1. Employee theft.   2.   Industry--Security
measures.   3.   Business losses.   I.   Title.
HF5549.5.E43H44   658.4'7   75-30944
ISBN 0-8144-5402-X

© 1976 AMACOM
A division of American Management Associations, New York.

First Printing

Preface

Loss PREVENTION programs have a new sense of urgency for the business community.

Preventive security is an inseparable aspect of most management practices, a thread that runs through the entire fabric of business.

This book was written to show why business losses occur, and how steps may be taken to control the erosion of profits and assets. Every company, of course, intends to make a profit. But at times it may be even more difficult to hold onto earnings than to obtain them in the first place.

The attitudes sometimes exhibited by management toward their products and merchandise seem hard to explain. At times, managers close their eyes to careless losses, waste, pilferage, and even internal theft. There seems to be little management concern that these lost or damaged items are as much company assets as money is that of a bank.

The examples in this book are intended to help management deal with the more common internal security and loss prevention problems that occur in almost any type of business. In the typical pattern, these conditions frequently give advance warnings that management should not overlook.

This material represents some of the impressions and experiences of a number of individuals in the loss prevention field, all men of unusual capabilities. I wish to express individual thanks to Jack R. Barbour, V. J. Bechtel, Art Beverford, Lee Chapman, W. E. Hawkins, Les Lobaugh, K. C. "Swede" Soderman, and D. R. Wardell. George R. Wackenhut and Don Richards provided encouragement, and Mrs. Margaret A. Morse was of considerable help in manuscript preparation.

CHARLES F. HEMPHILL, JR.

Contents

PART
1

APPLICATION of LOSS PREVENTION PRINCIPLES

Chapter
1

Loss prevention as a management philosophy

THE INCENTIVE FOR PROFIT has made American business the most successful enterprise system ever devised by man. Besides providing employment for numberless individuals, American business needs a profit margin for research and development of new products, for locating new raw materials and techniques, for lowering prices, and for repaying investors who risk their savings.

One of the positive results of the social turmoil of the sixties and seventies is that management is increasingly aware of the ways in which crime can affect the profit margin.

Crime is now at an all-time high in this country, while fear of punishment may be at an all-time low. Respect for authority in public life, at school, and in the home appears to be on the decline. Society continues to struggle with the question of the rights of an offending individual against the safety of the community.

Some of the street crimes, such as assault, murder, and rape, may not directly involve business, while crimes like armed robbery and burglary may have a direct bearing on business success or failure. Lawbreakers also strike at business through embezzlement, shoplifting, and many kinds of fraud. Some of these violations may involve merely pilfering candy bars from the company for consumption during the lunch break, or removing a single item from company stock that costs only a few pennies. While some of the more serious criminal offenses provide the most dramatic examples of this business problem, they may not be as costly in the end as the cumulative losses that result from the lack of management controls.

As business becomes more competitive, more ingenuity must be employed to stay in the race. Truly, loss prevention must be the business of business.

EMPLOYEE INVOLVEMENT CAN REDUCE LOSS

It is apparent that many business-loss problems center around employee misconduct. But in management's preoccupation with losses there is a tendency to see only the crime, the employee unconcern for shortages, the lack of care in handling merchandise. It is sometimes claimed that American business is accurately characterized by excessive profits, by shoddy workmanship, by repairmen who rip off the customer, and by labor unions bent on harming the employer. Distressed by a few dead trees, some businessmen fail to observe the basic value and beauty of the great stands of marketable timber that grow in between.

The truth is that most employees, when properly managed, obtain a great deal of satisfaction from meeting their daily responsibilities. Certainly some of these workers are discontented, and others find little challenge in their jobs. Yet on the average, the workforce has a great capacity to perform up to the standards that should be met. There may always be a certain amount of employee dissatisfaction, but this same quality often seems to drive people on to better achievement.

Some dreamers and far-out social planners talk of a society completely free of work. Under such a system all jobs would be handled by machines, with the inhabitants completely engrossed in leisure-time activities. All this loses sight of the fact that we are a nation of salespeople, cowboys, doctors, freight forwarders, deliverymen, painters, farmers, teachers, entertainers, and stockbrokers. Practically all these individuals find satisfaction in a job well done.

A generation or two ago there was more adherence to the ideas of the "old American work ethic"—work for work's sake. In recent years individuals have begun to question whether work without observable accomplishment is worth the effort. As a result of new attitudes, workers are often seeking something more meaningful than a job without measurable results.

This does not mean that employees as a whole are not inclined toward productive work. Management frequently overlooks the fact that company losses can be reduced or eliminated by devising controls and by involving employees in crime control programs that reflect accomplishment. Allowing employees to become involved in planning and implementation usually leads to improved morale and creativity.

This results not only in technical excellence in job performance but also in more employee efforts to protect the profits and reduce those conditions that lead to potential loss.

DEVELOPING A PHILOSOPHY TO REDUCE LOSS

Many companies simply do not make as much profit as management expects. Some make no profit at all. Frequently, this is because management mistakenly assumes that selling merchandise or services at a figure above costs will automatically result in a money-making operation.

Perhaps nothing is more frustrating for management than to believe that one has the formula for making a profit in today's competitive market and then see that profit all dissipated by pilferage or other criminal activities.

Stated in other words, anticipated gains may not be counted as certain until money is actually deposited in the company bank account. Even then, funds may be drawn off if controls do not protect against employee embezzlement.

Some companies have chosen to completely ignore problems of this kind. Others have merely taken note of the extra expense and have passed it along to the consumer.

In the typical pattern from the past, whenever a theft or other incident has come to light, management has tried to treat the specific incident, without isolating or correcting the cause. Usually, that has only compounded the problem. Thereafter, the problem has broken out in other areas of the business, and under other disguises, as losses continued.

Sometimes this has led to management concentration on the visible symbols of security: locks, window bars, chain link fences, guards, and alarms. That does not mean that all these other tools and techniques for controlling loss are not useful. They all serve definite business needs. But the most sophisticated technical devices available will not prove adequate if company employees cannot be motivated to become involved in a loss prevention program.

Increasingly serious losses have forced management to look to rank-and-file employees for assistance. Previously, businessmen had insisted that they needed only to rely on a security department to solve these problems. This is a resort to crisis management, a stopgap technique at best. Even if temporarily successful, a security program often results in action after the fact. But an effective loss prevention program can eliminate the damage before it occurs. In most instances it is far easier to prevent loss than to detect it in time to avoid a serious drain on the operating budget.

At times, companies have attempted to compensate for losses by increasing sales and productivity. The feeling here is that the most valuable individuals in the company are those responsible for marketing, sales, and finance. "After all," some managers say, "these are the people who bring in the money!"

But in recent years there has been a new approach to the problem. Employees in marketing, sales, and finance are, of course, primary movers in the company scheme of things. Undoubtedly, they are the employees who bring in the money. The individuals who participate in a loss prevention program are not involved in bringing funds into the organization, but they do succeed in keeping money in the company, sometimes a great deal of it.

It is important to turn new volume into profits. But it may be just as important to hold onto the funds already accumulated as it is to develop new sources of revenue. The focus here is to concentrate on preventive procedures, rather than to round up losses and to attempt recovery.

In many instances, management should examine the systems and procedures being followed, and where necessary institute new systems to minimize exposure. Such arrangements are often quite simple and need not be expensive or cumbersome. Too often, losses are accepted because individuals in management are simply not convinced that these losses may be avoidable.

What is needed is a system by which losses can be accurately pinpointed and causes determined. Thereafter, management should set up controls that make any attempt to alter the controls immediately apparent.

Loss figures provide a good management tool. Perhaps the most important factor in reducing losses is to develop a real concern about the problem among top operating management. The figures for loss experiences should be carefully analyzed. Do they indicate that significant changes are taking place? Is the ratio of losses to sales or merchandise handling on the increase? What is the particular type of loss that is developing most frequently? Is it pilferage on the loading dock, or missing packages when shipments reach the consignee? The first few incidents that are reported may be caused by accidents or unusual situations. If they continue, they are no longer accidents; they have become a part of the cost of doing business.

As soon as there is evidence that one particular kind of business loss is occurring frequently, the head of the division involved should investigate the causes behind each reported incident. If it will help, a management committee should be set up, with power to ask the necessary questions. What conditions brought about the loss? Are physical security controls and protective devices needed to prevent a reoccurrence? Are the systems and procedures that are in force being circumvented through poor supervision and through deliberate lack of concern by employees?

If it is determined that the deteriorating loss experience is a matter of poor warehousing or stockkeeping, management should take immediate steps to correct the situation. In instances when operating costs may be increased, it may be necessary to seek approval for these alterations through financial and budgetary controls.

An alert, efficient security department is, of course, of real value to any business. But in the long run, a practical, well-conceived loss prevention program that is implemented by employees may contribute far more to the profit structure.

Management should have a desire to prevent, rather than to be forced to detect, security problems! And prevention should be a thread that runs through the entire fabric of management responsibility.

A GOOD LOSS HISTORY DOES NOT
GUARANTEE IMMUNITY

The fact that a business has never experienced a serious loss does not mean that it is immune to the problems that plague other companies. If merchandise is attractive or useful to a customer, then it must also be worthwhile to a thief. It is undisputed that small, easily concealed items of high value are more likely to attract a dishonest individual. But if a truckload of merchandise is needed to make the theft worthwhile, then that is just what the criminals will steal—a truckload. And if employees leave keys in the company forklift, then the thieves will use the lift to make their job faster and easier.

USING A CONSULTANT

In making a survey of business vulnerability, it is generally preferable to utilize the services of an experienced loss prevention consultant.

Certainly no one individual can always foresee every possibility for loss that may exist in a business. But the objective view of an outsider, uninvolved with company procedures, may be of considerable value.

To illustrate what may occur, management at a large clothing manufacturer's warehouse was convinced that there were no loopholes in shipping procedures. What was happening here was that finished dresses and garments were being selected on sales invoices for distribution by truck to retail stores. After warehouse selection was completed, a checker verified the quantities and stock numbers of each item. Individual items were then placed in a locked truck bay until they were loaded onto the vehicle. As the merchandise was loaded onto the truck, an independent count was made by a truck checker. A truck manifest for each vehicle was prepared by the loader inside the locked bay, and was verified, item by item, by the checker.

A copy of the truck manifest was then given to the truck driver, while an additional copy of the truck manifest was mailed separately to the receiving store so that the contents of the load could be verified on arrival.

In observing this system at work, an outside loss prevention consultant observed that the truck manifest forms were prenumbered but were not numerically controlled. The possibility existed that a loader with access to uncontrolled truck manifest forms could prepare a second, fictitious manifest, recording only some of the dresses and garments that had been listed on the genuine manifest. If the fictitious manifest was inserted into the company's paper flow, and the copies of the genuine manifest removed or destroyed by the dishonest employee, there would be no record of the unlisted items that had been placed onto the truck.

By working with a dishonest driver, a thief could remove the unlisted merchandise en route from the warehouse to the retail store. There would be no way of knowing, of course, whether this kind of fraud would ever occur. But once a loophole of this kind is discovered, the fraud may be repeated, time after time. The problem could be solved by requiring accountability for each truck manifest by serial number, and keeping them under lock so that unaccounted-for manifest forms would not be available to the loaders. If a manifest should be unaccounted for, then an investigation could be immediately undertaken to determine what had happened.

It is my purpose to acquaint management and business employees with some of the ways in which a loss prevention framework can be set up. The organization may then develop and build to satisfy individual needs.

A good loss prevention program involves an interplay between a number of employees. Management needs an understanding of the systems to control the areas of likely loss, how to obtain employee acceptance and cooperation, how to motivate individual workers to be concerned about profit protection, and how to retain respect by insisting that company rules be followed without favoritism.

A loss prevention program does not offer solutions to all the troubles that may affect a business. It should be used to safeguard assets and profits, bearing in mind that a company profits from loss prevention as well as from sales. In most instances there is no way to keep statistics about the results that have been achieved, since the thrust of the program is toward losses to be avoided rather than recoveries that could be made.

Effectiveness should not be confused with sensationalism, since far more can usually be prevented than ever comes to the attention of management. Loss prevention is usually a quiet, unspectacular application of controls.

ASPECTS OF A LOSS PREVENTION PROGRAM

There are seven basic tasks to consider in planning and implementing a business loss prevention program:

1. Determining where exposure to loss exists.
2. Devising controls to eliminate or minimize these exposures.
3. Auditing the controls or procedures that have been put into effect.
4. Training employees in the need to cooperate in the program.
5. Conducting emergency investigative activity when controls break down; using the facts developed to make recommendations for additional controls that may be needed.
6. Keeping abreast of new techniques and newly perfected physical devices that will assist a program of this kind.
7. Conducting an exploratory inquiry into situations that seem to warrant suspicion, even though controls in this particular aspect of the business have not previously been considered necessary.

Chapter 2

Determining
loss exposures

THE PRIMARY GOAL of a loss prevention program should be to prevent the loss of company money, merchandise or materials owing to dishonesty, lack of concern, or error.

The failure to methodically identify and isolate exposures within the company in advance is one of the differences between the traditional security department approach and the loss prevention plan.

In determining the extent of losses, it is first necessary to admit that the problems may be more extensive than management suspects. Recognizing the potential for security losses is an exercise in specialized management skills. It involves an examination of the circumstances and factors that could contribute to loss, along with some understanding of the defensive measures to forestall them.

In setting up a loss prevention program, management should make a change in basic attitudes that are usually assumed. For example, when a company theft is first discovered, all attention is usually focused on learning which employee or other individual may have been responsible. In the typical situation, management officials are so disturbed that they can only react, rather than plan specific controls to handle such an incident in the future.

It is important, of course, to learn the identity of anyone stealing from the company. Management should determine the facts as soon as possible, thereafter discharging the responsible employee if warranted. At the same time, it should be realized that the theft incident called attention to a basic lack in the controls or that the implementation of existing procedures had broken down. The specific incident may not be as significant as the vulnerability it seems to underscore. It is a time when management should make certain there is a planned control program, set objectives, and match them to the capabilities of the business processes involved.

Extensive study and analysis of merchandise movement and the paper flow of the business are needed. A review of actual practices, as compared to management's version of what happens, may also be helpful. In short, the effectiveness of a loss prevention program requires a full understanding of the company's operation, and a clear methodology in meeting its objectives.

At times it may be found that the ingenuity and imagination of thieves may be greater than the imagination of the company defenders. What individuals in management sometimes consider to be an unlikely possibility for loss, and not warranting protection, is frequently found to be not only probable but, indeed, actually happening.

One of the first things for management to ask is, "Just what are our losses?" This question can, however, lead to self-deception on the part of management. If the company loss history involves numerous instances of problems, it would seem to follow that there should be a large budget for loss prevention. Conversely, if only a small number of losses are known, then it would appear that only a small budget would be justified. Unfortunately, business organizations often do not know the full extent of their losses. A statement of this kind can mean that only the exposed losses are low. Without practical, effective tests, a conclusion that losses have been small could be very deceptive.

In order to determine the likely areas for loss, management needs imagination and experience to make a list of potential problems. This should be done by individually examining each process or area in the business. A determination should then be made as to whether existing practices and procedures are already providing protection. If they are not, then management has isolated an existing exposure, and something should be done about it if costs of control are justified.

Too often, companies solve only the apparent or superficial troubles, overlooking the real problems that may be deeply submerged.

In analyzing business losses, accounting information should be considered as an important factor. Clearly, management must have confidence in the figures that indicate serious inventory shortages, prior to the time that company resources and management time can be committed to the prevention of problems in the future.

A prepackaged approach to all security problems may not be advisable here. Instead, management should strive for a system that allows for the use of some physical components or standard employee procedures yet remains flexible enough for the individual application.

Management must realize in advance that the solutions to loss prevention problems should be as complete as possible, but not restrictive. Systems that are followed should have the flexibility to meet day-to-day as well as special problems. At the same time, they must be capable of change or expansion to solve tomorrow's needs.

The costs of physical components for a security system can be spread over a period of time and depreciated as any other business expense.

A PLACE TO BEGIN

A practical approach to a loss prevention program should begin with a physical survey to point attention to the physical deficiencies of the business that make pilferage or theft easy, that make merchandise shipping hard to supervise, and so forth. The physical inspection should then be supplemented by an examination of the paper flow, of the procedural requirements that are used to bring valuable raw materials or merchandise into the business, and of the processes that are used in safeguarding, distributing, or shipping those valuables.

As a practical observation, the greatest areas of vulnerability will usually be found where assets or merchandise is physically accessible to unauthorized individuals, or where access can be gained by employees at low risk.

An approach that is sometimes used is to examine each department of the business separately, utilizing four questions, as follows:

1. If I were dishonest, what raw materials, money, or merchandise would be available here?
2. What procedures must be circumvented to remove valuables without immediate detection?
3. In the event the system could be bypassed or the controls manipulated, would this action be apparent to management?
4. Would supervision or management take action to determine what had happened in the event a deviation from the approved controls became apparent?

THE COMPANY LOSS HISTORY

Another way to begin is to examine the company's loss history. If management will go to the trouble to study specific previous losses, it is usually possible to pinpoint recurring problems that have not been corrected. Controls should then be considered for each individual problem. If procedures have not changed, it can be anticipated that similar losses may recur in the future.

If the company has internal auditors, it is likely that some problems have been described and documented in previous financial audits. This approach may be very helpful, since the internal auditor is expected to report variances from prescribed policies and to discover situations that indicate poor control practices.

Another way to start may be to review inspection reports previously submitted by the company's insurance carrier. Frequently these reports will be specific about problem areas or identify potential loss situations.

Another technique is to hold meetings with all employees, divided into groups of no more than 20 or 25. Individuals in these meetings may be given a blank sheet of paper and asked to submit a brief description of potential loss problems of which they have personal knowledge. Employees should be told that they do not have to sign the statements.

CATALOGING VULNERABILITIES

When a list of the company's vulnerabilities has been detailed, management should examine each individually. An assessment should then be made as to whether adequate controls are being used. Management may find that the controls are adequate, but that supervision makes no real effort to audit the controls or to correct the deficiencies found.

In some situations it may be necessary to devise a new form, or to add control copies to an existing form.

In identifying the loss exposures in the business, there may be several possibilities for applying effective controls. A cost consideration must enter into the assessment at this stage. Loss prevention does not come cheap. But the traditional security department approach costs even more, since the damage is done by the time detection comes into the picture. If a control system costs less than the existing problem seems to cost, then it is usually good business to insist on the use of controls, at least on a spot-check basis.

FREQUENCY RATE ANALYSIS

A frequency rate system may be used to determine where company losses are taking place. For example, a warehouse superintendent in

Chicago devised a simple, card-sized form to record responsibility for each error that was made in selecting warehouse merchandise to be shipped. These cards were accumulated for a month. A study of the cards then revealed that some merchandise selectors had made no errors that were detected by the checkers who recounted orders being placed on delivery trucks. Other selectors, however, were found to have made errors frequently. The findings indicated that some merchandise selectors were so error-prone that they should be transferred to other types of jobs or that they did not realize the possibilities for loss.

Using a frequency rate application, management has a tool to evaluate which employees should be counseled and which workers do not have the dependability to perform adequately in this sensitive job.

WHAT TO INCLUDE IN A
LOSS PREVENTION PROGRAM

The problems to be considered in a loss prevention program will vary from business to business, depending on exposure areas, local problems, and the type of business or industry. It is suggested that the loss prevention program be set up in three broad areas:

1. Personnel security as it relates to the selection and motivation of employees to avoid loss.
2. Physical controls.
3. Procedural controls.

The review of personnel practices should include the following:
Applicant evaluation systems.
Background screening methods.
Training and motivation of new employees and retraining of existing personnel.
Exit interviews to determine problems and viewpoints of employees.
Emergency action plans.

The physical aspects of loss prevention should include the following, at the minimum:
Night lighting.
Parking lot controls.
Perimeter barriers and fences.
Ingress, egress, and access controls and procedures.
Key control and lock analysis.

Personal safety of employees and property, including vehicles, accessories, and gasoline supplies.

Employee identification systems.

Utilization of security guards.

Vendor controls.

Janitorial and maintenance service problems.

Scrap and trash disposal procedures.

Building alarms and access control systems: fire protection and alarm systems.

Assessment of vulnerability by area.

Locations possibly exposed to theft, sabotage, or business espionage.

Computer location and security.

At the minimum, it is recommended that procedural controls consider the following:

Purchasing.

Receiving.

Shipping.

Invoicing.

Returned goods.

Transfer of raw materials and finished products within the plant.

Product inspection and rejection methods.

Identification and classification of proprietary information.

Inventory controls over raw materials supplies.

The accumulation, separation, and sale or use of scrap or side products.

File and retention procedures.

Computer data control and protection of computer files.

Destruction of unneeded file data.

Control of mailroom procedures, long-distance telephone calls, and copy-machine costs.

Chapter 3

Setting up controls to prevent loss

EXPOSURE TO LOSS exists within the structure of almost every business. Facility layout designs and physical controls are almost always helpful in eliminating or restricting unnecessary losses. But the procedural controls or paper-flow systems that must be set up and followed are usually more important than other considerations.

PHYSICAL CONTROLS

The emphasis on procedural controls does not mean that physical devices and controls should not also be used. In selecting physical control systems, it is usually advisable to follow the advice of someone who is well acquainted with physical security techniques and the results that can be expected from specific installations.

To get down to cases, closed-circuit television installations in a warehouse, bank lobby, or retail store may be of great value in some applications. In other installations, however, it may be apparent that the lighting is not sufficient to produce a satisfactory picture on the TV monitor. Or the mobility of the camera may be so seriously impaired that it cannot be used to scan a wide area. After spending the money for a satisfactory TV installation, some companies have found that they cannot justify the continuing expenditures needed to keep cameras and receiving monitors in sharp focus, along with the continuing expense that every TV installation entails—an employee who has the time to devote almost complete attention to the monitor, if the installation is to be of much value.

PROCEDURAL CONTROLS

If properly devised and implemented, good controls will promptly alert supervision or management to deviations from normal activity patterns. It is then up to management to determine why the situation is abnormal. An effective program must also rely on a sustaining inspection and audit system, to insure that the procedures are being followed.

Just what kinds of controls should be worked out by management to eliminate or make difficult the opportunity for employee embezzlement or theft? There is no universal answer. Controls must vary from industry to industry and from company to company. There are times when different applications should even be considered between stores in the same retail chain, although in most systems there are a number of benefits from companywide uniformity.

The procedures recommended should represent sound management principles and should incorporate the basic controls essential to the operation of the business. Sufficient research and analysis should precede the adoption of every control recommended by management or a loss prevention consultant. If controls are subsequently found to be unworkable, time may be wasted and the result may be loss of respect for management.

Two basic ideas should be considered in setting up procedural controls. One or the other of these principles will usually be effective in a wide number of applications.

Principle number one

Basic Separation of Responsibility

In the handling of money or merchandise, the basic function should be conducted by one employee, with independent verification and record keeping by another.

Stated in other terms, the employee given custody of money or valuable merchandise should not be the same employee who maintains records of the receipt or disposal of money or merchandise.

This principle goes back to the idea that there should be a separation of responsibilities between employees. A high percentage of employees are honest, and it can be expected that they will remain so. But in any business there may be exceptions. It is quite unlikely, however, that two previously trustworthy employees will agree to become involved in dishonesty at the same time. A potential thief will usually avoid temptation if he knows there will be independent verification of his stewardship.

In applying this principle of separation, accountants and auditors have long recognized that the cashier of a business should not also serve as the company bookkeeper.

In like manner, one individual in a business office should have responsibility to deposit or withdraw bank funds, while a second employee should have sole responsibility to reconcile the bank account.

Similarly, one employee should be responsible to maintain accounts receivable records, while another office worker should verify the accuracy of these records through contacts with the customers represented by these accounts.

The following are examples of this principle.

If a cash register is used to record sales receipts, the register should not be balanced by the same employee who uses it to record sales.

A salesclerk in a retail store usually has authority to accept returned goods from a customer; however, each transaction of this type should be verified by a supervisor or member of management.

If a warehouse superintendent is allowed to sell scrap metal as salvage, then there should be independent verification of the weight and quality of the metal that is hauled away.

In a stockroom area, one employee should be entrusted with the job of storing and retaining merchandise under his control. A second employee, working independently, should keep records of goods received and disposed of.

Maintenance of a perpetual inventory system enables company officials to detect inventory shrinkage almost immediately and to take corrective action as soon as the shrinkage is discovered. Here again, there should be complete separation of responsibilities. Shipping and receiving employees should not be allowed to post records to the perpetual inventory system since a loss in the warehouse or stockroom could be covered up if a dishonest person from the shipping or receiving departments were allowed to post a nonexistent transaction in the inventory records.

In a recent case in Chicago, an insurance manager for a large corporation defrauded his company by use of a fictitious invoice submitted on a dummy insurance firm. In another, somewhat similar situation, an insurance broker defrauded an insured by issuing and collecting for a policy without actually placing the business. A situation involving frauds of this kind would be detected by proper application of the separation of responsibility principle. This would involve verification of policies purchased by an employee other than the insurance manager, and by verifying coverage directly with the insurer.

In a small or medium-size company, one single individual may have responsibility for compiling the firm's payroll. Actual cases prove that the person handling this job may place a "ghost" on the payroll, causing the issuance of an extra paycheck that may be cashed by the payroll clerk. Unless a situation of this kind is detected, it may continue for years. And in some cases, more than one ghost may be placed on the payroll.

Under the separation of responsibility principle, it is suggested that one person continue to have the responsibility to compile the payroll data. As an audit of this procedure, a second employee should pass out the paychecks, requiring each employee to identify himself and pick up his check in person.

In a recent incident in Miami, Florida, it was found that a check collection manager had secreted large sums of money given to him to pay off "insufficient funds" checks. If the separation of responsibility principle had been applied here, the collection manager would not have had authority over the checks entrusted to him, as well as responsibility for all funds collected. The fraud could have been prevented through independent verification by a second employee making contacts with a representative number of persons responsible for giving those checks to the company.

Some companies have found that verification of these collections may not be justified from a cost standpoint. This would, of course, involve a management decision. The controls would be valid in any event.

Whenever management needs to tailor loss prevention controls to a specific exposure problem, this basic principle of separation should be employed.

It does not matter whether the risk to be controlled involves avoiding loss of cash receipts in the office or on the sales floor, or whether the problem involves control of merchandise in transit, in a wholesale warehouse, or in a retail outlet.

Some businesses may have so few employees that they cannot use the separation principle. It may be necessary for one worker to handle a number of different functions. The same kind of control weakness may be found in small branches of a large business, where the hiring of additional employees cannot be justified. When a situation of this kind is encountered, it is suggested that management conduct general audits more frequently at these locations. Opportunities for embezzlement are sometimes greater in a branch location than in the main office of a business. Usually, there is more supervision at company headquarters, so more frequent verification is suggested for those locations where employees perform multiple duties.

Separation between the handling of merchandise or money and the verification of transactions should be used by management whenever possible.

Principle number two
Reduce Access to Money and Merchandise.

Reduce access to money and merchandise, insofar as practical, with regard to both the time frame and the number of persons involved.

This may seem to be an oversimplification, since a retail merchant cannot sell goods without displaying merchandise to the customers. But at the same time, the merchant would not grant uncontrolled customer access to his stockroom or warehouse.

Some gasoline service stations in high-crime neighborhoods have adopted a policy of making sales at night only to holders of credit cards or of insisting on exact-cash transactions. When cash is received for gasoline, it is placed in a locked box by the station attendant, who does not have a key to open the cash register. Armed robbery is pointless when the business operates under a system of this kind. Access to company receipts has simply been eliminated.

A somewhat similar approach is that of requiring a cashier to operate within a specified cash limit. When the limit is reached, excess cash must be immediately deposited in a bank. This procedure may utilize an armored car service to come by daily to pick up bank deposits. There is still some exposure as long as operating funds are kept on hand, but the possibility for a holdup is reduced considerably. There is simply less access to company money and less temptation to a professional criminal.

The manager of a St. Louis restaurant noticed that his waitresses were consistently pocketing their tips. There was no objection to this practice, but it was then learned that waitresses were also concealing customer checks in their pockets, along with small sums left at the counter to pay these checks. The manager solved this problem by furnishing each waitress a tip cup that was located behind the counter, as well as an attractive wraparound apron without pockets. Deprived of a pocket to conceal customer checks and company money, the waitresses began bringing all money and customer checks to the cash register. In effect, management had cut off access to company funds.

A Kansas City, Missouri, tobacco and cigarette wholesaler followed the recommendations of a loss prevention consultant, who recommended closely restricting warehouse access to necessary personnel only. The wholesaler later reported:

> We still allow manufacturers representatives into our warehouses, but only after checking in our front office verifying with the manager that they may go into the restricted area, and having someone accompany them at all times. They go in through the office and go out through the office. If any merchandise whatever is released to them, it is taken out by our employee charged with filling will-call orders, and subsequently approved by the warehouse manager. Our warehouse inventory has been in balance ever since we started this system.

It was apparent in this instance that losses stopped when access to valuable merchandise was restricted to only a few, responsible employees.

A somewhat similar problem was encountered by a New Jersey firm that manufactured a single product—plastic garden hose with solid brass couplings. On a number of separate occasions thieves stole sizable quantities of brass couplings. apparently for the salvage value of the brass. The plastic materials and the nylon reinforcing thread used in manufacturing the hose were left behind.

A loss prevention consultant recommended that the boxes containing brass couplings be locked in a large cage, with a single key available to the foreman in charge of each shift. After this recommendation was acted on, a logbook was used to record all withdrawals and deposits of brass.

Production in this manufacturing operation could be figured very closely, and a procedure was followed whereby the shift foreman removed sufficient couplings for his shift, with this stock placed in full view of all the extruder machine operators and hose assemblers. In an emergency situation the shift foreman could obtain additional couplings, and this action would be apparent to almost all the employees on the shift. After this system was instituted, the losses ceased.

THINKING LIKE A THIEF

In setting up procedures, it may be advisable to examine each control from the viewpoint of a potential wrongdoer. For example, in Reno,

Nevada, a store manager believed that employees might be tempted to steal high-value items such as electric shavers, binoculars, portable radios or handguns from warehouse stock. He therefore worked out a procedure for placing railroad seals on the hasps of lockers used to store expensive stock items. The warehouse superintendent regularly examined the seals and always found them in place, with no evidence of tampering. It was therefore assumed that unauthorized persons had not been in the lockers. At inventory time management was surprised to learn that there were serious shortages in high-value items.

A loss prevention consultant made a survey of this facility shortly thereafter and found that the warehouse superintendent stored his supply of railroad seals in an unlocked drawer in his desk. It was then apparent that anyone who knew where the seals were kept could break the existing seal, remove merchandise, and substitute a new seal from the uncontrolled supply in the superintendent's desk.

REPLACEMENT COST DETERMINES
NEED FOR PROTECTION

Some companies do not regard assets worth protecting unless those items have considerable resale value. In observing the activities in a cigarette warehouse, it was discovered that a roll of cigarette stamps, costing $3,000, was not locked up at night or afforded protection when the warehouse was open. There was always a possibility that the roll could be lost in the trash, or deliberately carried out by a disgruntled worker.

This situation illustrates the idea that protection should be based on replacement cost rather than on resale value on the black market or at a pawn shop.

EMPLOYEE OPINIONS ARE VALUABLE

In developing controls for a business, management should make certain that the lines of communication to its employees are open. At times it may appear that a proposed system would work well, but it is usually advisable to consult those employees who may be most familiar with the way that controls would function in actual practice. It is better to know the objections to a proposed procedure prior to forcing it upon employees, who know of conditions that make it unworkable. Management is not seeking to run a popularity contest in devising company systems, but it helps the morale and enthusiasm of employees to consider their views.

WRITTEN PROCEDURES INSURE EFFECTIVE CONTROLS

When controls have been decided upon, the next job is to reduce them to written procedures. Management is likely to understand the instructions that are intended, but this may not hold true for members of the staff, subordinates, and the people that management wishes to instruct.

Quite frankly, the language used in some procedures is dull and verbose. Some instructions miss the mark, and in a few companies they are rarely updated.

A written procedure should be simply a document that outlines the controls that are to be followed, in other words, instructions that tell employees how to go about doing their work. Procedures must be specific and clear if they are to be used and if they are to achieve their basic objective—constructive action.

For clarity, accuracy, and employee understanding, all orders except the most menial should be in writing.

Chapter 4

Auditing the controls

A LOSS PREVENTION survey is not an automatic panacea to the problems of business. When a survey is made, it is up to management to do something about the problem uncovered or to ignore it. And even after controls and written procedures are set up, it is necessary for management to follow up with an effective auditing program. Unless management determines whether the controls are enforced, employees will not take them seriously. Even poorly conceived systems, conscientiously followed, will usually prove more effective than well-conceived procedures that are haphazardly applied. In effect, a prevention program is no stronger than the audit methods that it utilizes.

Internal dishonesty has many faces. Whatever form it assumes, some variance from normal patterns must appear. It is to these variances, these signals, that management must be sensitive and must react.

CONDUCT REGULAR, UNANNOUNCED AUDITS

Inspections, or audits, should be conducted regularly, but at unannounced times. Much of the effect will be lost if employees always know when and where management will seek to verify controls.

Employees should understand that audits of actual adherence to procedures are directed at the system rather than at any specific employee or group. Supervisory personnel must be made responsible for auditing, and it is important that all findings be reported to top management.

AUDIT ALL SHIFTS

Audits of control procedures are more likely to detect significant omissions during the second or third shift, or during overtime periods. This may be due, in part, to the fact that employees and supervision may not be so alert when working overtime or at late hours.

To illustrate what may happen, the manager of a Chicago distribution center recently made an unscheduled audit of shipping procedures on the second shift. His suspicions had been aroused when he noted a loaded truck parked at the shipping platform, with no supervisors in the vicinity. The manager ordered the truck unloaded and the shipment compared with delivery documents. It was found that the boxes on the rear of the vehicle were legitimate shipments, but approximately one-third of the merchandise that had been loaded onto the truck was not accounted for in the shipping documents.

The warehouse checker, who was responsible for verifying each package loaded onto the vehicle, was found asleep and the driver of the vehicle had placed considerable additional merchandise in with his own load.

Some companies consistently use good controls for shipping warehouse merchandise by parcel delivery service. A practical auditing technique here involves verification of the package counts with the sales orders or shipping documents on hand.

Before the Christmas season it is not unusual for some companies to allow a breakdown of these controls. "After all, we would stand in line all day," is the employee argument usually advanced, "if we had to send these by Parcel Post." When employees are allowed to use these forwarding facilities, the only cost to the company may be the shipping clerk's time.

Actual losses, however, may be otherwise. Businesses that have made this concession to employees have found that they were not being paid for charges or that the shipping clerk was pocketing the cash given him for the payment. Then, too, there is always the possibility that employees who are allowed to wrap merchandise in the warehouse may include company items in their own packages.

In any event, employees may waste considerable time in wrapping on company time, when they should perform these chores at home. Admittedly, losses of this kind are usually relatively small. They may not affect company profits greatly, but shipping and merchandise controls can usually command better enforcement if they are at least inflexibly applied.

In auditing shipping procedures, another method is to feed deliberate errors into the system. The auditing technique here is either to remove merchandise from a shipment that has been selected or to add additional merchandise and then observe whether the shipping clerk will allow the order to go out without verifying the quantities. In some instances the shipping clerk has attempted to place the extra merchandise into his personal vehicle, parked outside the building, or to turn it over to a truck driver with whom he is in collusion.

Another auditing technique is to withhold a billing invoice and then determine whether the missing invoice number will be reported or ignored.

USE MATHEMATICAL PROBABILITY

It is desirable but not absolutely essential for management to audit every transaction involving a possibility of embezzlement or theft. Sometimes the verification of a representative number of transactions can provide reasonable controls, without entailing the cost of complete audits. This is not to say, however, that management can afford to downgrade the auditing function.

For example, companies in the industrial uniform rental business are sometimes plagued by drivers who submit false credit invoices. What happens here is that a dishonest driver may claim that he did not deliver a set of clean uniforms to a service station or other customer along his route because the customer was on vacation or was home sick. The driver had, in fact, taken other uniforms out of company stock and had delivered and had collected for the uniforms. He then pocketed the cash.

Some companies use customer representatives (supervisors) to verify claims of nondelivery. As a practical matter, some supervisors close their eyes to these frauds since they do not realize the full extent of loss.

If the textile rental company processes 1,000 refunds a year through office accounting, the probability of locating one of these false credits would seem to be small. However, by taking advantage of mathematical probability, an auditor can test only 2 percent of the total cash credits and have a 50 percent probability that one or more false items will be detected. If the auditor checks 5 percent, he will have an 85 percent probability of locating one or more of the phony credits.

In using a probability auditing technique, management must ask two questions: (1) How many false items in a given situation would mean a serious problem or systematic theft? (2) How accurate does management want to be in this test? For example, management may have accumulated 100 cash credits in a month and may feel that a serious problem exists if there are more than 10 fraudulent refund slips in the 100. Management may also decide that a discovery test that offers a 65 percent probability of detection would represent all the auditing effort that should be devoted to the project.

In the probability chart shown in Figure 1, the number of "false items" is indicated next to each curved line. The degree of probability is at the left side of the chart, and the percentage of items to be tested is shown on top of the chart.

In the auditing plan selected by management, it will be found that allowing for ten fictitious credits and insisting on 65 percent probability, it will be necessary to verify 10 percent of the credit invoices by contact with the individual customers. These test items should, of course, be selected at random. If, after auditing 10 percent (ten of one hundred), there was no disclosure of any fraudulent items among the ten chosen at random, then it is likely that there are less than ten fictitious credit items in the total group of one hundred. If the auditor did turn up one or more fictitious items in the samples selected, then by management's set of standards there is a serious theft problem. In that event, it may be desirable to verify each invoice submitted.

The probability chart is satisfactory for all groups of test sampling of between 100 and 1,000 or more items. It will be noted that the probability of discovery increases in direct proportion to the number of items involved.

Management may find that there are several problems in a company that could be disclosed by this simple method.

AUDIT SALESMEN'S SAMPLES

Frequently, inventory shrinkages may correspond to the number of visits that company salesmen make to the warehouse. Many salesmen frankly admit that they pick up samples to be left with customers and that this technique is usually beneficial to the sales program.

On the other side of the picture, some companies have been

Figure 1. Probability chart.

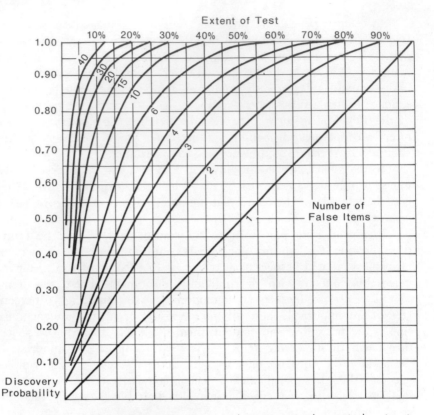

1. Decide how many fictitious items you consider serious in the particular situation under study (using "6" as an example).

2. How accurate do you wish this test to be? (Choose odds of three out of four in your favor, or a 0.75 discovery probability.)

3. Locate the point on the chart at which the arc representing six errors crosses the horizontal line representing a 0.75 discovery probability and read off, from the top of the chart, the percentage of the group that must be checked.

surprised to add up the cost of samples that have been given away by salesmen. To what extent samples should be used is obviously a management decision, and not within the scope of this discussion. Failure to control access to samples can, however, result in considerable loss.

There is often a difference of opinion between employees as to the extent to which salesmen pick up samples from the warehouse. Typically, when interviewed, salesmen state that this does occur, but rather infrequently. Warehouse employees definitely feel that it is fairly common for salesmen to go into the warehouse, especially after night meetings or sales meetings when the warehouse may be unsecured and unattended.

It is suggested that sales employees be escorted whenever they go into the warehouse. There are several advantages in this procedure. Inexperienced salesmen frequently take down stock for examination and return it to the wrong shelf. They remove items without making notations on the master merchanidse box, and they may remove samples for a customer who accompanies a salesman into the warehouse.

In addition, the salesman may receive an emergency telephone call and leave the customer unattended. Some customers have been observed pocketing high-value merchandise. It is therefore recommended that sales employees and customers be escorted into the warehouse and that salesmen be instructed that they are not to pick up merchandise without proper paperwork to account for the disposition of samples.

REPORT TO TOP MANAGEMENT

It is important that the employee auditing loss controls should report only to upper management. For example, if a security representative must report to a store manager, it is possible that significant information may never reach top management. Recently in Los Angeles an internal auditor learned that a customer had not been credited for funds that he claimed to have paid. Investigation revealed that a company collections manager had been making sizable cash collections and pocketing the proceeds. The collections manager was operating on the belief that the accounts were soon to be written off as uncollectible, and that he would never be called to account.

A restricted chain of communications could have made it possible for the collections manager to furnish the local store manager with the monies collected. In that case, the facts may never have come to the attention of top management. Reporting of each breach of control should be direct to officials at the upper level.

UNDERCOVER AGENTS

Some people feel that there is something morally wrong in the use of an undercover operator in business. Everyone resents being spied on, but there is nothing private or confidential about the on-the-job activities of an employee. Management has every right to know what goes on within the company. This obligation to be informed is completely separate from an intent to pry into the personal activities of employees away from work. Apart from the job, management has a right to know only those things that are public and that indicate a lack of honesty or fitness handling the job. Management need make no apology in keeping abreast of activities and working conditions inside the business.

The type of material that may be obtained through an undercover agent is almost unlimited. In attempting to improve employee relations, information may be developed as to moral problems. Management may find proof of employee dealings with business competitors, falsification of company incentive or pay records, and production slowdowns.

An undercover program may have wide application, but it will not automatically eliminate all management problems. Controls must still be devised and implemented. Companies that profit from the adoption of an undercover program must still use appropriate caution.

If it should be revealed through accident or carelessness that an undercover man has been used, relations between management and workers may be damaged. To avoid embarrassment for management, it is often desirable for the entire operation to be handled through a reputable security firm or investigative agency.

Placing the secret operator on the job is often a delicate operation. Companies that have considerable employee turnover generally experience fewer problems. Frequently in industry the personnel manager also serves as safety and security director, and placement will be easier if this official can be taken into confidence. If security must be absolute, the undercover agent, with management supervision, must gain employment on his own ability. This may mean that the security firm must send several potential employees before one is accepted.

The undercover person must be willing to perform whatever work is necessary to hold the job rather than to rely on his or her arrangement with management. If the secret agent has a better background than the job demands or has less than the basic skills needed, the other employees will be suspicious from the outset. The agent must neither overplay nor underplay the part.

An undercover operator can seldom gain the confidence of co-workers at the outset. The results expected by management may be slow in coming, but an experienced agent is worth the time necessary to spot employee dishonesty.

In a wholesale drug warehouse an undercover operator noted that one of the employees had a number of larger-than-average pockets sewn into the lining of a trench coat. Focusing attention on this one individual, the agent observed that the owner of the coat carried out large quantities of expensive drugs. Eventually, the thief was arrested after police officials were called into the case. Drugs worth about $40,000 were recovered from his garage.

Written reports

Verbal reports from the operator are not as valuable as written statements. Written reports should be submitted daily, and explicit facts must be included. For security reasons, it is desirable to mail these communications to the home address of the company official who has the contact with the undercover agent.

At times, the information developed cannot be used without exposing the identity of the operator. If the agent's cover is blown, employees may try to get back at the company.

Briefing the agent

The quantity and quality of information reported by the undercover operator usually depends on the amount of time spent in the briefing sessions. At the minimum, the operator should be given basic information concerning company policies, security rules, and procedures for handling money and merchandise.

Usually, the faster the undercover agent can complete his or her assignment the better the chances that the employees will not get wise to the true purpose of the mission. It may only be a question of time until the operator is faced with a chance encounter with a former acquaintance and his or her real background exposed.

The close of the working day may be the most difficult time for the undercover agent. This is when co-workers may want to stop for a glass of beer and a friendly chat, and the agent must use this opportunity to develop close contacts with them.

One of the problems here is that the undercover man may ask for more and more "beer money" to be compensated for these late hour contacts. Requests of this kind must be evaluated on an individual basis, depending on the value of the information received. Unless activities are properly supervised, undercover operators may request increasing amounts of money for expenses.

Broader aspects of undercover programs

At times, employee performance varies widely from the policies and procedures that have been specified by management. The real cause for a breakdown of this kind may be hard to identify. The problem may be that management is seriously out of touch with employee thinking and response.

To function effectively, the executive must keep a finger on the employee pulse. Often, rank-and-file workers know the answer to a specific problem but are cut off by supervision when they attempt to communicate. If the organization structure isolates management, top-level decisions may be based on inadequate information.

What management needs, of course, is an open line of communication from the bottom to the top. If this channel remains uncluttered, productivity and quality remain high, employee morale works for the company good, and labor disputes and work slowdowns are not so likely to occur.

Experience demonstrates that an internal intelligence type of listening post, at a working level inside the company, can provide specific, meaningful information on which management decisions may be based.

A number of security companies provide undercover operators for management on request. But their activities are traditionally directed toward identifying an internal thief, or learning about an employee who is addicted to narcotics. This type of undercover work is of course valuable, but it provides only a few of the answers that management can use. By expanding the scope of the undercover operation to that of internal intelligence, considerably more could be obtained.

Management needs to know which policies are working successfully and why others are not accepted and implemented by employees. The top executives should also be informed as to what continuing support may be needed in other specific areas.

Some companies rely solely on the employee grapevine to be informed. The usefulness of this management tool should be acknowledged, but the information received through it may be distorted or may represent wishful thinking on the part of a small number of employees. Then, too, the material received through this source is frequently negative in nature.

In some instances it may be only the manager's ego that blocks the introduction of an intelligence operator in the working level of the company. In making use of an employee of this kind, the manager must be mature enough to look at his own administrative practices objectively. He must take constructive criticism impersonally, realizing that it is directed at the operation as it exists. The manager who is willing to utilize an undercover employee to identify an internal thief should be able to broaden the horizon of the operator to isolate weaknesses in the systems and procedural aspects of the business.

Management should realize here that the primary object of the internal agent is to let top management know how the business is being run, not how to run the business. It is only when management really knows what is taking place that meaningful remedial action can be taken.

PART
2
EMPLOYEE PROBLEMS

Hiring and retaining dependable employees

Two MAJOR ASSETS of any company are loyal employees and loyal customers. A market-oriented company works constantly to help customers solve their problems. In like manner, management must work to select loyal, honest employees and to make sure that employee integrity is ongoing.

In the final analysis, the quality of the man that is hired, along with management's handling of him, is all that will lead to success.

From time to time, management may improve the physical devices used to restrict access to the premises. Stronger safes may be provided and doors and windows equipped with more sophisticated locks and other hardware. In addition, management may call in a consultant to make certain that systems and procedures are being followed in accordance with specified security objectives.

Regardless of the kinds of physical and procedural controls that may be installed by management, their effectiveness may be compromised by poor security performance on the part of employees. The individuals who are hired, then, are a major ingredient in any loss prevention program.

But it is usually a mistake to hire and fire employees at will, or to make wholesale transfers of personnel. Efficiency, productivity, and morale may suffer if employees are changed like security hardware. It is essential—and common sense—that the proper employees be hired in the first place.

This is not to say that the effectiveness of procedural controls and physical hardware is completely at the mercy of the employees. But it does mean that the overall program may be sharply devalued if unreliable employees are used to put cash register receipts in the company vault, to make certain that the building is locked, or to protect merchandise in the warehouse. In short, any company needs honest human beings to operate the protective devices and management controls that have been set up. Management should, of course, also be concerned about the work performance and promotional potential of a new employee, but not to the exclusion of honesty.

It may be an oversimplification, but it can be anticipated that internal losses will correspond to the general level of honesty of the individual employees. Attitudes of individuals at the working level are very important. Management should therefore realize the necessity to create an environment for honesty, in which each individual wants to be part of the program. It cannot be overemphasized that motivation of individual workers will do more to create a loss-free environment than any other factor.

With the assistance of the loss prevention or security department, management must seek to create a healthy environment.

THE HIRING PROCESS

Hiring should not be done under "panic" conditions. An appropriate background check of an applicant, prior to hire, is basic. Some companies allow an employee to begin work before a background check is made. The idea is that the individual is on probation for 60 or 90 days and that the investigation will be completed in the meantime. If information should be developed to reflect on the integrity of the employee, there is a natural reluctance to take action against the new hire. "After all, he's doing a satisfactory job, so why rock the boat?"

Because management may be reluctant to take action on any derogatory information developed, some individuals are allowed to remain on the job despite a questionable background, and may find themselves in a position of trust.

This does not mean that a person with a questionable background cannot be an acceptable, honest employee. Statistics from bonding and insurance companies spell out a convincing argument, however, for exercising care in the hiring process. Every individual has basic rights and human dignity, and no one should ever be deprived of the right to earn a living. On the other hand, no company should be forced to hire an applicant for a sensitive job after that person has demonstrated by past performance that he may be untrustworthy.

The hiring process is but the first step in which individuals enter the company and work up to positions of greater responsibility. The continued financial success of the company may be closely interwoven with its ability to recruit talented employees and to motivate them to good performance. But performance and potential for in-company advancement may not be the most important criterion for hiring.

Stability and dependability

Sometimes a worker may behave in an unstable or irrational manner without causing loss to his company. Nevertheless, stability is a key ingredient in selecting employees who are good security risks.

Business companies are not looking for dull, unimaginative employees, but the unpredictable individual may cause many problems. Figures maintained regarding in-company losses reflect that individuals with unstable activity patterns may be more apt to be involved in theft, embezzlement, or other internal business crime.

It is, therefore, important for the personnel department to make probing inquiries to ascertain the applicant's stability. Fellow workers, neighbors, and former employers can usually supply this information. All the interviewer is looking for is the truth. He is not trying to discredit any applicant. To the contrary, he is trying to fill a job position as quickly as possible.

If questionable areas are found in the applicant's background, that does not indicate that he has been a criminal in the generally accepted meaning of the term. If the applicant's marital or personal life reflects serious problems, then he may be under pressures that frequently indicate a lack of dependability. Dependability, it must be emphasized, is almost always the controlling factor. A bad credit record, constant absenteeism, and inability to stay with one job may be important. Drinking too much and running up charge accounts are other factors that indicate a lack of dependability.

The personnel department that hires the applicant is almost invariably looking for personal discipline. If the applicant can discipline himself in the outside world, then the chances are excellent that he will adjust to the job and meet its challenges. Bankruptcy or unnecessary debts are all unfavorable indicators. If the applicant has a tendency to live beyond his income, he does not have the discipline that is needed.

Almost everyone runs into an unanticipated need for money at some time or another. This may be because of serious, unexpected illness, or misfortune beyond his control.

Also, a poor attitude toward marital responsibilities may indicate serious instability. Divorce may or may not reflect adversely on the applicant. But a failure to care for small children would seem to be a serious defect.

In the changing social structure of the modern world, it is not unusual for a job applicant to list a number of prior addresses over a short period of years. A generation or two ago, it was unusual for a stable person who paid his bills regularly to move frequently, but this factor may no longer be controlling.

Questions about financial obligations, prior employment, and family status should help to weed out some undesirables. But these questions are helpful in most instances only if the answers are verified by the employment office. It may also have some psychological effect to ask the job seeker to sign a printed agreement, stating that falsification will eliminate the applicant from consideration without recourse against the employer.

As previously noted, experience shows that applicants who frequently change residence are often trying to avoid bill collectors. It is therefore helpful to determine from the applicant whether there were other reasons for each move.

It is usually desirable to make a routine credit check of every employee. But if a bad credit record is found, it is suggested that the applicant be afforded ample opportunity to explain his credit problems.

Some of the other characteristics of an individual may be revealed by an in-depth check by the personnel office. Former employers and supervisors can often give good insight into the abilities and qualifications of an individual, as well as his weaknesses. If inquiries can be made on a personal basis, then acquaintances and former employers are far more likely to disclose the applicant's unfavorable qualities along with his good qualities. When the job seeker is asked to bring his own letters of reference, the record will most likely be completely favorable to the applicant.

If written inquiries are relied on, it may be well to note that most former employers praise more freely in a written communication than when they describe the former employee in a conversation. Often, people are afraid to be completely candid, since they may fear that the written record could someday serve as a basis for a lawsuit against the writer, regardless of his honest opinion.

As a final note, management has the responsibility to insure that each employee is matched to his or her job. An individual should not be put in a position where he or she is forced to lie or cheat about job performance because of inability to perform assigned tasks.

DISCRIMINATORY PRACTICES

The employer is basically interested in using hiring practices that eliminate security risks. But he should be careful to avoid discriminatory practices in achieving this result.

The Civil Rights Act of 1964 prohibits any business hiring policy that discriminates because of race, color, religion, sex, or national origin. Under Title VII, this law forbids not only overt discrimination but also employment policies that are fair in form but discriminatory in operation.

The Civil Rights Act of 1964 is not a criminal statute. Police officers or government agents are not authorized to arrest anyone for refusing to comply with its terms. The remedies under this act are by civil suit for damages against the employer or by an injunction against the employer.

If employment statistics show considerable disparity between the company's workforce and the racial balance in the general population, then the Equal Employment Opportunity Commission (EEOC) may demand that the imbalance be corrected by the hiring of minorities.

In the past many companies throughout the United States followed a policy of rejecting any job applicant who was found to have been arrested or convicted on a serious criminal charge. No distinction was made between persons who were charged with a crime and those who were actually convicted.

The EEOC has taken the position that on the average blacks are arrested far more frequently than whites and that this is a fact of life in the big city ghetto, due to the conditions of life and to police harassment. The commission also asserts that there is no evidence to uphold a claim that individuals who have not been convicted, but have been arrested on a number of occasions, can be expected to function less honestly or less efficiently then others on the job. The commission therefore takes the position that an arrest is merely an accusation and that a black person cannot be excluded for arrests alone.

This simply does not square with the loss experience records of bonding companies. In criminal prosecutions in this country a man has always been presumed innocent until actually convicted. But few companies want to trust their money and assets to an individual who has been charged with a serious offense on several occasions even though he was never convicted. A person who is repeatedly under strong suspicion of a criminal violation does not usually find himself in this position through unfortunate circumstances alone.

Because of the backing that the EEOC has received from the federal courts, it is recommended that employment applications should inquire only as to convictions, ignoring questions about arrests.[1]

A firm may legally require specific educational background or other restrictive qualifications—but only when there is a showing that it is related to job performance. If the position clearly requires a high degree of skill, and if the human and economic risks are considerably increased by hiring individuals who do not meet the prescribed qualifications, then the employer can be highly selective. He cannot, however, refuse individuals who do meet those standards. For jobs that require only a small amount of experience or training, the courts can be expected to find that any preemployment tests or requirements that screen out one race or group of people will be struck down.

Accordingly, a firm that does not want to be handicapped with security risks and incompetents should set up job standards in advance for sensitive positions, making sure that these are justifiable under the job requirements. Then anyone fitting those standards should be hired regardless of background, race, or other group classifications.

As a generalization, any question on a job application form is improper if it seeks to draw out information about race, sex, religion, or ancestry for discriminatory purposes. If the employer is an aircraft manufacturer, engaged in choosing fighter aircraft pilots to test an experimental plane with an unusually small cockpit, then questions as to the height, weight, and manual dexterity of applicants would be proper. Questions that specifically relate to the restrictive requirements of a skilled or unusual job are not objectionable.

[1] There are a number of court decisions that relate to the use of an arrest record as a hiring criterion: Gregory v. Litton Systems, Inc., 316 F. Supp 401 (1970), later modified in 472 F 2d 631 (1972); Carter v. Gallagher, 453 F 2d 315 (1974), and modified in 452 F 2d 327 and 406 US 9550, in which further appeal was denied.

If the job requires a high degree of trust, then the employer may refuse to hire an ex-convict. A hotel, for example, could decline to hire a convicted criminal as a bellman who had access to guests' property. The same employer could not, however, decline to employ the same individual as an elevator operator transporting the bellman and the guest's bags.

The inclusion of marital status information is also opposed by some on the grounds that a married woman could be likely to miss work because of pregnancy and the employer would therefore not want her. Similarly, the argument can be made that the number of children a woman applicant has should not be asked. This would be on the basis that a company might discriminate against her because she may have excessive absences to care for children in times of illness.

If background information is developed to indicate that a minority applicant is of questionable reliability, it is suggested that sufficient time be given to the applicant to explain away this information. Maintenance of a log of cases of this kind may be useful in showing that the company is seeking to comply with government regulations while attempting to hire employees who would protect the company's money and assets.

EMPLOYEES' PERSONAL PROBLEMS

Personal problems and pressures frequently motivate employees to become involved in theft. If managers and supervisors are sensitive to changes in behavioral patterns, problems may be solved before they reach serious proportions. Waiting until excessive drinking becomes evident, marital problems become acute, or job interest and productivity lessen may be too late to help the employee. Often these conditions are preceded by individual changes that may be apparent to someone in authority. Guidance at this stage can sometimes help the employee to get back his self-respect before he commits a dischargeable offense or a serious crime.

Chapter 6

Motivating employees to protect profits

EMPLOYEES ARE FREQUENTLY unconcerned about the financial success of the company that hires them. Too often, their attitude is that the company has been in business for years and will continue without interruption. "After all, any firm that's got so much money invested in it shouldn't have any worries!"

Whether employees like to think about it or not, thousands of American businesses do fail every year. Concerns that were once prominent on the business scene are unheard of today. Without earnings there will be no company, and in the private enterprise system the making of a profit is the only way to guarantee survival as well as company growth.

If employees are so unconcerned that they do not look out for the company's products or money, they are asking for trouble for themselves as well as for the company. If they assume the attitude, for example, that pilferage is a fringe benefit of their employment, then their acts will have a noticeable impact on profit margins.

There are both managers and workers who simply do not realize that the American profit system works for the betterment of both employees and company. In part, this may be because these people have not had an extensive background in economics. Some may simply be critical of business for ideological reasons.

Managers should let workers know that the company not only is entitled to make money but is completely dependent on profits to continue to provide jobs. It should then be brought home to employees that a business can remain competitive only by exerting efforts to control waste, product abuse, burglary, internal pilferage, and theft.

When employees are properly motivated to look out for the profit objective, they can expect job security, raises and promotions, and personal satisfaction in their work.

It is in the interest of the business community to correct some of the erroneous impressions that employees sometimes repeat: that businesses automatically make money simply by reason of the fact that they are in existence and have a large investment, that business profits are usually unreasonable, that businesses prefer to "gouge" rather than serve the public, and that a little pilferage won't hurt the profit picture.

THE EMPLOYEE'S ATTITUDE

Figures compiled annually for a number of years by leading bonding and insurance companies indicate that about 30 percent of all business failures are caused by theft, embezzlement, or serious product abuse by trusted employees of those companies. Losses of this kind are occurring daily in many industrial plants, retail and wholesale firms, and in business offices. Losses also occur frequently when goods are in transit. But despite this growing tendency, losses can be eliminated or controlled.

Too often, workers simply do not directly relate their own attitudes and activities to their company's performance. Most of these individuals think of themselves as completely independent of the organization for which they work. In effect, however, a company is nothing more than the total of the efforts of all its employees. What each individual and his fellow workers do on a day-to-day basis determines whether the company is a winner or a loser.

Losses attributable to one individual worker may not seem to have much significance, but the cumulative total may be considerable. When these conditions are eliminated, employees at all levels gain additional job security and the opportunity for advancement.

Some managers and supervisors believe that employees should be closely tied to their assigned tasks—in other words, that the company should look only to the security department to maintain security. These same company officials sometimes feel that there is no need to motivate anyone else to look after money or merchandise losses or even material waste. They fail to realize that employees should be taught that security requires some concern by every person who wants the company to make a profit.

Stated another way: It should be brought home to rank-and-file workers that any improper action, or failure to act, may lead to loss. And taken all together, these losses may jeopardize the jobs of everyone. Basic company loss figures are usually related to the performance and integrity of the individual employee.

Experience in case after case has demonstrated that it is usually easier to hold onto profits by concentrating on prevention. The opposite approach, of course, is to conduct a great deal of investigation after a loss has been discovered.

MOTIVATION BY SUPERVISION

Management's contact with the rank-and-file employee is frequently through first-line supervision, so supervisors should be trained in loss prevention responsibilities.

When a supervisor tries to motivate individuals to prevent loss, he is not trying to manipulate their personalities. The most effective motivation comes from within the employee himself. What, then, is the supervisor's role?

First, it is up to the supervisor to create and maintain an atmosphere in which honesty is respected and employees want to do a good job.

Then, too, the supervisor should assume that all workers are honest. Most employees will respect high standards if they are presented in a proper way. And management and supervision should let every employee know what those standards are. Also, officials should get across to employees that every individual is expected to meet those standards.

It should be understood that there is no single way to motivate employees, to the exclusion of other methods. Research, however, lends more support to the business leader who involves employees in a participative style.

By allowing individuals to feel a part of the organization, a manager draws upon their knowledge, keeps his or her staff informed, and is aware of their attitudes and desires. For their part, employees tend to feel more secure. By understanding security problems, they can interact with managers and fellow workers in group discussions and in problem solving. Not only are losses reduced; there is increased job satisfaction.

MANAGEMENT'S EXAMPLE

There is good reason to believe that some business crimes are unlikely to occur in the absence of management acquiescence. Sometimes management acquiescence is latent, sometimes it is obvious. In any case, employees seem to know almost instinctively whether management will take a stand or whether dishonesty will be condoned.

Since employee attitudes are frequently molded by example, it is important for management and supervision to be scrupulously honest in attitudes toward individual employees and toward the company at the same time. A supervisor cannot afford to be honest in his own actions while he ignores or ridicules company security regulations that are somewhat restrictive.

If a person in management does not agree with a specific regulation or policy, then he should work to bring about change. He should never allow adverse feelings to become known below the management level, however, because this serves to encourage workers to oppose any and all rules that they do not like.

Ethical codes are of little use if they are left hanging on the wall. They must be put into practice by supervision and management. Dishonesty should be unmasked whenever possible, and supervisory offenders should not be protected because of their position.

It is also worth noting that the business hustler is sometimes pictured as a kind of folk hero in today's culture. This type of individual should be debunked and exposed for the kind of morality that reflects on business.

INSTRUCTING EMPLOYEES

Management should encourage supervisors to demonstrate methods that can be used to hold down needless loss. For example, a supervisor can teach techniques to avoid shipments of the wrong kind of merchandise, or that eliminate overshipments or undershipments. The supervisor can also point out basic problems and solutions; for example, thefts from the company dock may be eliminated by bringing high-value goods inside the warehouse at the first opportunity after these items have been received from the delivery truck.

Whatever the type of business, the supervisor should demonstrate basic protective procedures for handling company merchandise and money. If there is any question, the company should seek the advice of an experienced outside consultant on specific procedures.

GIVING EMPLOYEES CREDIT

Good managers usually have considerable confidence in their employees. Asking for information and soliciting suggestions from workers is undoubtedly a valuable tool. The manager who displays trust is more likely to receive it from his subordinates and to obtain effective compliance with security rules and procedures.

Managers should also encourage supervisors to give credit to individual employees who carry out security procedures in a businesslike manner. It is helpful for the individual worker to receive specific, constructive criticism if he falls short of his obligations. If praise and criticism are both constructive, they may aid in making a climate of cooperation. It is usually harmful to give out undeserved praise, but it is effective to make clear to everyone that the supervisor has confidence and pride in his crew.

KEEPING EMPLOYEES INFORMED

There should, of course, be a definite purpose behind each company security procedure.

It is therefore important to keep individual workers informed about some of the details of security and how the company program works. This does not mean that management should pass out confidential information, or run the risk of being sued for disclosing that a specific person was discharged for theft. But people have a tendency to resent the discipline that goes hand in hand with security, unless the need for company rules is understood. When the reasons behind a regulation are explained, better compliance can usually be expected.

An uninformed worker, for example, may not be sympathetic with a company rule requiring the removal of the ignition key from a company forklift which is not being used. Understanding the rule could result by relating an incident in which a neighborhood high school boy suffered a badly crushed leg while trying to operate a forklift that had been left unattended on a freight dock near the school.

In addition to regretting the serious injury that resulted to the student, the company might be subjected to a costly lawsuit as a result of this accident. The whole matter would have been avoided by observance of the company rule.

It might also be explained to the employee that a costly burglary sometimes results if the forklift is left in an operating condition when the warehouse is closed for the night. Burglars may use the forklift to quickly load company merchandise and drive it away on a truck.

GETTING EMPLOYEES ON THE TEAM

Most employees are, of course, quite knowledgeable about their job responsibilities. Not only should all employees be made aware of security needs, but they should also be told that management relies on them to protect the interests of their company. Good security usually follows, almost automatically, when management and supervision are regarded as being on the same team with employees. The key word is "we," not "they."

Management can also give people more responsibility, more freedom to make decisions regarding their particular activity. Every firm needs objectives and overall goals. But as soon as these have been clearly defined and approved, workers should be encouraged to work out their own systems for reaching these objectives.

Individual employees are often motivated, not so much by specific monetary rewards, as by feeling that they are a part of a successful, needed program. Motivation sometimes comes from allowing individuals to utilize their unique talents, and by recognizing achievements.

Many companies have gained acceptance and implementation of a loss control program through meetings with small groups of workers. Part of the program here is for management to make a sincere expression of confidence in people. When employee awareness is created, many individuals will take pride, even find stature, in seeking ways to protect company profits. They want to work for and be a part of an organization of recognized honesty and integrity.

Abilities seem to blossom under encouragement in a climate of respect and confidence, but wither under unjustified fault finding by supervision or management.

Other employer–employee problems

TEMPORARY EMPLOYEES

IN RECENT YEARS, temporary employees have been used all over the United States to bridge the gaps caused by employee absences. Considering the differences in working in unfamiliar, diverse businesses with a wide variety of systems, many temporary workers have been a credit to their agency. Nevertheless, continued use of temporary employees may place some added strains on the loss prevention program of a business. This may be especially true if the business ships and receives large quantities of valuable, easily concealed merchandise.

In a southwestern city a temporary employee stole a number of transistor radios from an appliance warehouse. Because there was no supervisor, the temporary employee made repeated trips to a brush-covered vacant lot behind the warehouse, taking a radio or two with him on each trip. He concealed his thefts by stacking the empty radio boxes neatly on the warehouse shelf. Several weeks after the temporary employee had pawned the radios and left town, the thefts were discovered during an inventory.

This single incident points out five factors that should be considered:

1. It is often a questionable practice to allow employees to enter or leave a merchandise storage area or warehouse without supervision.

2. Merchandise boxes on a warehouse shelf may have been stripped of their contents, so the presence of the box is not a reliable verification of an inventory stock count.
3. A regular employee should be assigned responsibility for the supervision of a temporary worker.
4. Temporary employees should not be assigned loading, shipping, or receiving duties involving small stock items of unusual value.
5. The temporary employee often has no permanent contacts through which he can be traced in the event he should be wanted for questioning about theft or other serious crime.

Qualifications of temporary employees

Some authorities on employee security believe that stability (dependability) may be the most important employee trait that an employer may seek.

In many instances, the temporary may have areas in his background that point to the fact that he may not be a reliable worker. He may be unable to hold a steady job because he is a confirmed thief who will take either money or merchandise. Possibly he drinks excessively or uses liquor on the job. There is also a good likelihood that he is a drug user who may be accident-prone, damaging merchandise or causing serious injury to co-workers. Harm of this nature can, of course, result in a costly lawsuit against the company.

This does not mean that all temporary workers are of questionable honesty, loyalty, or ability. Some may simply lack the ability to sell themselves in the labor market. Some may have other reasons to choose flexible working hours—such as students, parents, writers, and people in show business. In time, these individuals may go on to become regular employees. It is suggested that they be processed through the established company employment procedures.

Some examples of loss

Two men who were hired through a temporary agency were assigned to work in an area of the warehouse that was considered relatively "sterile," or immune to theft.

On the afternoon of the same day, the warehouse superintendent walked around the exterior of the building making a visual inspection of the railroad spur track alongside. That was a required, regular company security procedure. While conducting the examination, the superintendent noted a loose wire protruding from a steel roll-down warehouse door. Investigation then indicated that the temporary workers inside the warehouse had "wired around" the warehouse door so that it was no longer included in a warehouse alarm system. They had also removed the screws from the hasp that was used in padlocking this door. Apparently, the warehouse containing a large stock of colored TV sets had been set up for a costly burglary.

Realizing the potential danger, the warehouse superintendent quickly slipped away to an outside telephone to arrange for a police stakeout. However, he had already alerted the culprits to the discovery, so the stakeout was unproductive.

Supervision is essential

One way to effectively control temporary employees is to assign a regular worker the responsibility for the temporary individual. There are times, of course, when this is simply not practical, especially if the duties involved can be performed by one man. On the other hand, one company man may be able to supervise the activities of two or three temporary employees in unloading merchandise from a boxcar. In these cases it is necessary that the regular employee understand that he must bear responsibility for those assigned to his supervision.

In Philadelphia recently, a temporary worker picked up the warehouse superintendent's keys when they were carelessly left in a shipping-desk drawer. As soon as he was able to do so, the temporary worker telephoned an acquaintance, who came to that location, carried away the "borrowed" keys, and had them duplicated. The keys were then returned without anyone else being aware that they had been missing. Subsequently, the duplicate keys were used to provide access in a burglary.

In Chicago, a temporary warehouseman noted that door padlocks were left hanging unlocked (unsnapped) on a warehouse door hasp. When he was subsequently reassigned to this location, he came supplied with a used padlock of the same kind. Substituting his own lock for that of the company, the temporary worker controlled the key to the padlock that was used to secure the warehouse door at closing time. Instead of leaving the premises at the end of the day, the temporary employee hid in a company rest room. After nightfall, he made his exit from the warehouse with considerable merchandise.

A temporary worker in Denver managed to unbolt a locked basement window and gave access to his accomplice, who later entered the premises in the middle of the night.

At the very least, management can be selective in the kinds of duties it assigns to nonpermanent workers. If there is a high-value area in the warehouse, it should remain off limits at all times.

Some businesses frequently use part-time workers supplied by agencies without even recording the identity of such persons. It is suggested that each nonpermanent worker be identified in a company log by driver's license number, Social Security number, birth certificate name, or whatever other valid identification may be available.

If feasible, temporary employees should be furnished a temporary badge, complete with photograph and identification. The badge should be taken up at the end of the working day.

Some companies have gone so far as to require temporary employees to sign a form giving consent for the warehouse superintendent to search the worker on his departure from the premises. At those companies, such consent is a prerequisite to employment. A search of this kind may be legally valid, if the consent was voluntarily given. But such a requirement for temporary employment could be regarded as degrading, and there is no certainty that the courts will always look on it with favor.

In any event, management and supervision should realize that uncontrolled utilization of temporary employees could cause problems in minimizing merchandise loss.

EMPLOYEE PURCHASES

Perhaps the majority of retail stores in this country allow their employees to purchase company merchandise at a substantial discount. In addition, some wholesale firms allow this privilege, while companies that provide only services may let workers purchase tools, supplies, or equipment that is regularly maintained in stock.

Purchases of this kind usually seem to be a factor in building employee morale. Furthermore, there may be somewhat less of a tendency toward employee theft when workers are able to purchase a desired item at a good discount.

A Hollywood, California, cosmetics factory carried employee benefits one step further by furnishing women workers with a free kit of personal cosmetics at regular intervals. This donation was appropriately treated by most employees, but management eventually discovered that a few people were taking additional kits for their relatives and friends, and for sale to the general public. When it was learned that greedy individuals were taking advantage of this wind-fall, the company discontinued the practice for everyone.

A minority of companies flatly refuse to sell to employees at a discount, pointing out that there is a tendency to abuse the privilege, and that the additional work required to handle these transactions does not justify the effort.

When employees are allowed to make purchases, it is not unusual for them to select their own items, sometimes on the honor system. Frequently, this leads to loss. It can be expected that an employee will not place extra items in a customer's package, although he may slip additional articles into his own sack. While not confirmed criminals, employees are only human and may not be able to resist taking advantage of a poorly controlled system.

In Kansas City not long ago, a supervisor detected one retail clerk selling merchandise to another at five cents on the dollar. When confronted with this observation, both clerks admitted that they rang up sales at reduced prices when it was unlikely that the floor supervisor would be on the sales floor. This is a typical form of dishonesty that occurs frequently. It may be eliminated, or reduced considerably, if company policy requires all sales to employees to be verified and approved by a member of management or supervision.

An additional item occasionally slipped into an employee's purchase package may not bankrupt any company. If repeated frequently, however, the drain may be costly. Some companies allow the individual to take his wrapped purchase to his own work area. If the purchase is placed in a sack, it may be secured with a hand stapling machine. This precaution is of doubtful value from a loss prevention standpoint, since it is usually easy to insert additional items into the sack.

Some companies require supervisors or department heads to make selections of merchandise or to require a purchase list to be submitted in advance. If a reasonable deadline is set, the merchandise may be selected by a stock clerk and the orders packaged by a supervisor. One satisfactory variation of this method involves retention of the employee purchases at a central control point until the worker leaves for the day.

It is only common sense to forbid the employee to take his package back to his own work station. It is also desirable to locate the pickup point for employee purchases as near as possible to an employee exit door. Then a company policy should be in effect prohibiting the worker from reentering the building. This is for the employee's protection—to remove him from suspicion—as well as in the company's best interest.

Auditing employee purchases

It is desirable for a member of the auditing staff to insure that proceeds from sales to employees actually get into the company coffers. In the New York City area, a business executive sold appliances and expensive household furnishings to employees at a discount. Because of the executive's position, no one questioned whether he handled the sales through regular channels. An internal auditor eventually learned that none of these sales was ever reported and that the executive collected installment payments from the purchasers. There were so many of these transactions that the executive kept a separate set of books. In the end, those records contributed to his downfall.

Selling "seconds" to employees

Defective or shopworn merchandise cannot of course be sold to a regular customer. But something may be salvaged by a sale to an employee.

Experience shows, however, that supervisors sometimes abuse their authority to mark down a defective article, letting it go to an employee at an unreasonably low price. It is also rather common to find that employees deliberately deface merchandise that they wish to buy at a markdown sale.

Some companies have also discovered that repairmen are slow to replace damaged components that would make an appliance or other article capable of being sold as new.

Also, considerable employee time may be lost while salesclerks and warehouse employees ignore their assigned duties to look for items that may be subject to sale at a distressed merchandise price.

Because of all these factors, some companies refuse to sell seconds or damaged items to employees. The attitude generally expressed here is that an entire accumulation of damaged merchandise should be sold to the highest bidder. Other companies junk the whole lot, first making sure that the individual items are smashed or rendered unusable. Some give merchandise of this class to a charitable organization, to save time and handling costs.

Employee charge accounts

Some companies encourage employee charge accounts, desiring the added volume of sales. One of the hazards here is that the employee may destroy his own charge slip, if he is able to gain access to it. If this should occur, the accounting office will never be aware that the employee should have been billed.

Two types of controls may be helpful in preventing loss in this situation. First, charge tickets should be handled as carefully as cash, being retained in the cash register or company safe until charged to the employee's account on the company books. Second, all charge tickets should be numerically accounted for, so that management or the accounting office will be alerted if a ticket should be fraudulently removed from the office paper flow.

EMPLOYEE ACCEPTANCE OF A LOSS PREVENTION PROGRAM

Most employees will readily acknowledge that there is a definite purpose in enforcing company systems and procedures. As long as loss prevention and security requirements are uniformly applied, they are generally accepted.

It is important that a double standard not be used by management in enforcing violations of company rules. Managers, supervisors, and office workers should be treated the same as individuals in other jobs. If a company rule specifies that automatic discharge is the penalty for a violation such as theft, then in fairness to everyone, it should be uniformly applied. Some companies make exceptions for employees in management, or for employees who appear to have unusual promise, but in the end the organization suffers. If the incident is a criminal violation and the company policy is to prosecute, management must remember that *no* employee is above the law.

FAMILY-OWNED COMPANIES

Two cousins in Dallas, Texas, owned and operated a company doing approximately $4 million business a year. Each partner drew $17,500 a year in salary. Both drove luxury automobiles and lived in expensive homes. Each of them spent four weeks hunting in Mexico each year, as well as two weeks in Arizona during the winter. That kind of living could not be done, of course, on $17,500 a year.

Considerable quantities of scrap copper, brass, and aluminum were accumulated in the company's production area. This scrapped metal was sold to a salvage company, and checks were issued to the business. The two partners endorsed the checks in the names of their firm and added their own names. These checks were then taken to the bank and converted into cash, with no record of the transaction ever appearing in the company books or the partners' tax returns. This side income totaled about $35,000 a year for each of the partners.

One of the sidelights to this story is that office employees usually reported to work about 9:30 or 10:00 o'clock. The hour that was allowed for lunch was seldom respected. Quite often stenographic and clerical employees had left for home by 4:00 or 4:30. There were eight employees on the office staff and in an indirect manner, all of them were taking advantage of their knowledge of the partners' schemes for lining their own pockets.

The truth is that in abusing the business, management destroys the respect that individual employees have for company assets. Such a situation is more apt to occur in a small, family-owned business, but the basic idea is the same: Management must act as a steward of company assets, just as it expects the same honesty from each employee. If the individual workers observe that management has no respect for the company, its time, and its assets, they ask, "Why should I be concerned holding down losses or reducing costs if the boss doesn't care?"

VANDALISM

There is nothing really new in the problem of vandalism, the willful and pointless defacement or destruction of property. The word itself came into modern language from the fierce, invading tribe named the Vandals, who wrecked almost everything in the city of Rome in A.D. 455. Every generation has had to contend with some senseless destruction, but never on the scale recorded in recent years in the world's richest nation.

No section of the United States has been immune. Perhaps the bulk of this criminal activity has been directed against public facilities, schools, parks, transportation buildings, and institutions. In any given year, assaults on this country's schools result in damage estimated at about half a billion dollars. It is not unusual for poor students or individuals with emotional problems to set fire to the school building on a weekend or at night.

But business and industrial facilities have suffered also. For no logical reason, a group of California youths recently broke the lock from a railroad switch, which inactivated an automatic derailing device and disabled the brakes on a tank car filled with inflammables. With brakes inoperable, the tank car rolled from the siding onto the main line and crashed into a switch engine. Fire broke out immediately, and two railroad employees were killed.

A writeoff of the property itself is only part of the cost of vandalism, which is perhaps outweighed by outlays for increased security and guard protection, those costs that accumulate when a plant is closed, increased insurance charges, and loss of customers. Some companies and government agencies include the costs of vandalism in with the costs for regular maintenance of buildings and facilities. Often, it must be reckoned as pure loss to the business.

One of the troublesome aspects of vandalism is the lack of certainty or predictive factors in determining the time and target location of any hostile action directed against physical property.

Criminologists and authorities on juvenile behavior are frequently at a loss to explain the kind of behavior that is involved. Some feel that vandalism is a result of the social tensions in the modern world: racial unrest, unemployment, family instability, and lack of social and religious ties. Others believe that it is antisocial behavior resulting from permissive attitudes and lack of discipline in the home, the school, and society in general. Authorities point out that in many instances the individuals involved cannot offer any explanation for their acts.

Perhaps most acts of vandalism outside business buildings are perpetrated by juveniles, but damage inside a business establishment may be the work of disgruntled workers. When a leading automobile manufacturer closed down a plant at the end of 1974 because of a lack of orders, employees responded by smashing a number of valuable patterns and mock-up devices as they left the plant. The workers did not make any complaint against the company, but somehow they seemed to reason that it was the responsibility of the company to keep them employed, whether or not there was any business.

A Chicago food-producing company was recently crippled by a series of four fires in the production area of a main building. The first of these three incidents caused little damage, but the fourth was so extensive that the entire production of the plant was shut down for about two months. Long-standing customers were retained only because the company was able to bring in merchandise from a plant in the Pittsburgh area.

From the location of these internal fires it was apparent that they were started by an employee or an ex-employee who believed he had a grievance.

Management could have taken a warning from any one of the early fires and ordered the installation of automatic water sprinkler systems throughout the plant. Because of the cost, management declined to do so until after the fourth fire. It should be pointed out, however, that most water sprinkler systems may pay for the original cost outlay within a few years in lowered insurance premiums.

Police and arson investigators have never been able to pin down responsibility for these fires. Thus the plant is vulnerable to additional outbreaks unless access to company buildings is carefully controlled and accountability is maintained at all times for all persons in specific areas of the company property. A revision of the guard system appears to be indicated, along with changes for all keys and locks. In addition, lack of controls in the perimeter has always allowed access to all inside areas of the property. Consideration should therefore be given to either locking critical areas that are not in use or patrolling these areas effectively. Frequent clock rounds by alert guards could also prove helpful in spotting intruders and fires.

Protection against graffiti

Almost every company wants to present a good public image. In recent years there has been a considerable increase in scrawled slogans and obscene signs on exterior walls and in the rest rooms of business buildings. An invisible coating of paintlike material can now be applied over wall surfaces, allowing graffiti or signs to be wiped off immediately with soapy water or solvent. The coating material reduces loss in maintenance because of the activities of outside gangs or employees inclined toward vandalism. This material is now sold through specialty paint stores.

INEFFICIENCY, CARELESSNESS, AND WASTE

Sometimes serious loss may be caused by nothing more sinister than lack of concern. Waste and inefficiency may also cause serious problems unless management concern is made evident.

A loss prevention consultant at a major airline discovered that a large quantity of new ball bearings had been placed in a trash dumpster. At the time, it appeared that the ball bearings were being concealed by a thief who had located a sale for them on the black market. Discreet inquiry revealed, however, that the goods had been deliberately dumped into the trash bin by the stockroom supervisor.

Asked why he had done this, the supervisor said that he was short of storage room. He also said that he could no longer identify individual ball bearings by serial number since his catalogs on this merchandise had been lost. He then decided that the entire lot, costing over $10,000, should be thrown out.

Management immediately ordered the recovery of this merchandise from the trash dumpster and disciplined the supervisor for careless waste. Within four hours all the bearings were identified as replacement parts for specific aircraft engines after a supplier's catalog was received.

Chapter
8

Setting rules and standards for employees

SOME EMPLOYEES actually do not know what kind of performance is expected of them. Others may want to know just how serious the company is about protecting merchandise and cash. Experience shows that compliance with the company's policies is generally better if workers know that definite restrictions are in effect and that management intends to apply the penalties that have been specified. Accordingly, it is important to make the company policies known to all employees.

By incorporating security rules, the employee's manual is a useful tool for communicating these responsibilities to everyone. If manuals are not readily available, employees may be able to claim that they were not aware of the rules and should be excused for violations. Some companies therefore furnish a manual to each employee. Others issue manuals to employees who request them. One effective way to bring the manual to the attention of workers is to attach a copy to each company bulletin board. Drawings and illustrated slogans may also be used.

In addition to including company rules in employees' manuals some companies incorporate security and safety rules on one or two sheets of paper. At the time of hire, each new worker is required to read and sign the list. The list is then permanently retained in the employee's personnel file.

After the employee has been on the job from two to four weeks, it is recommended that the sheet of security rules be reviewed with him. This review is far more likely to make an impression on the worker, since he may have signed so many forms and papers on the first day that he can't remember them all.

It is also valuable to discuss safety and security regulations at companywide meetings, as well as for supervisors to remind the individuals who work under them. If these techniques have been used to spell out company rules and penalties, there is considerably less likelihood of disputes that may result in labor arbitration.

Lists of company regulations are of little value if they are not understood. In Southern California, Texas, Arizona, and New Mexico there are large numbers of Spanish-speaking workers who have a passable knowledge of spoken English but can read only Spanish. It is important that government regulations and company safety and security rules be clearly posted in as many languages as necessary.

WHAT ACTIVITY SHOULD BE PROHIBITED?

At the minimum, it is recommended that there be a company rule against theft, with immediate discharge as the penalty. In addition, employees should be advised that the company reserves the right to request prosecution for this activity. Pilferage of merchandise should also be prohibited.

It is also recommended that the company have definite rules against drinking on the job, reporting for work while under the influence of liquor, or bringing liquor onto the premises at any time. This prohibition should also extend to the company parking lot.

A similar rule should be in effect pertaining to narcotic or dangerous drugs, or any type of knife, gun, or other weapon.

It should also be made clear that fighting on the premises will not be tolerated, and that employee horseplay is also forbidden because it could result in serious liability for injury.

Employees should also be advised that they may be subject to discharge if they punch in or out for another worker on the company timeclock.

Another rule that should be considered by management is the requirement that employees are to use only a designated entry and exit door. It may also be helpful to clearly point out to employees that company storage lockers have been provided for convenience and that everything in the lockers continues to be company property, except for personal-convenience items placed there for employees. It is suggested that employees be advised the company reserves the right to go through these lockers from time to time and that the employee accepts use of the locker subject to this control.

If an employee is discharged for any reason, it is good policy to notify the company guard. If employee identification cards issued to this individual have not been returned, it is suggested that the identifying numbers of these items also be furnished to the guard.

The guard should be instructed that he is not to let these discharged individuals into the building after hours or on the weekend and that under no circumstances should he allow them to remove files, equipment, or articles that they claim as personal property unless they have a pass signed by their supervisor or other member of management.

RESPONSIBILITY OF THE SECURITY DIRECTOR

There are times when the director of loss prevention and security may need to define his authority and responsibility in a company manual or other publication. The following material could serve as a model, when applied to the individual requirements of a specific company.

It is essential that the company continue its operations, profitably, with the least possible loss of interruption from illegal activities or undesirable influences that may properly be avoided.

In order to maximize profits, the company has employed a director of loss prevention and security. This position was instituted and developed to fill the need for a special service-type department that would be available to set up preventive programs and to handle the investigative needs of the entire company, working with other ranking officials.

Preventive programs and investigative problems must necessarily be coordinated by the director of loss prevention and security. Preventive security as such, however, is not a separate and distinct responsibility of the department. It is so closely aligned with good management practices as to be inseparably linked with overall managerial competency. It is therefore essential that other departments of the business work closely with the director of loss prevention and security.

To hold losses to a minimum, a security representative will automatically enter into and investigate incidents that appear to involve possible financial loss to this company and its affiliates. Any official of the company may request the services of the loss prevention and security department at any time the known facts warrant such a request.

The functions of this department are not intended to supplant in any way the administrative or executive responsibilities of the various operating departments or of the individual supervisors who discharge administrative duties normally assigned to them. The loss prevention and security department has authority to investigate any incident or set of circumstances that indicates that this company or its affiliates have incurred, or might incur, financial loss under circumstances that indicate dishonesty, thievery, or embezzlement.

The loss prevention and security director has authority to recommend procedures to individual departments for the control of loss. For their part, individual executives and administrators should work with this department in installing and making effective those controls that can be expected to insure honest performance from all employees.

Insofar as efficiency can be maintained and costs kept within workable limits, the recommendations by the director of loss prevention and security should be followed, both for actual controls and for theft deterrents.

In addition, the director of loss prevention and security should have authority to audit and conduct verification examinations of those procedures set up to control loss from dishonesty, embezzlement, waste, or lack of concern for company property. Upon notification, a representative of the loss prevention and security department should proceed as soon as expedient to conducting necessary investigations and to auditing security procedures. In all instances, however, it will be incumbent upon the director of loss prevention and security to keep top management advised of developments that reflect on the integrity of individual employees or of the control processes being used in the business.

If it becomes apparent to the director of loss prevention and security that company procedures have loopholes that may be used by dishonest employees, then it shall be his or her responsibility to make recommendations that will eliminate the weakness.

When an employee is believed to have defrauded the company, the major department head concerned will be immediately advised of developments in his own department. In all cases, when the matter first comes to the attention of company personnel, a security investigator of the company will, where available and in accordance with established procedures, be immediately consulted, and his advice and assistance sought. Upon the arrival of the security investigator at the scene of the suspected or actual violation, he or she will have complete charge of the investigation, subject to frequent consultation with the executive vice-president or other management official designated by him or her. The security investigator will conduct operations and proceed with the investigation to ascertain whether there is a weakness in company procedures and to determine the identity of the specific individual responsible. Upon determining the existence of a weakness, the security investigator will make a recommendation for whatever changes in procedures may be warranted by the facts developed. In all inquiries and investigations, the director of loss prevention and security will receive the active cooperation of all company personnel.

In the event a security investigator of the company is temporarily unavailable and the situation is of such urgent or emergency nature as to appear to require the immediate presence of the law, the ranking company official should have an appropriate call made to a police officer. Upon the arrival of the officer at the scene, the situation should be explained to him, but the actions of the officer should not be directed, nor should he be told what to do or how to accomplish it. Help to the officer should not be volunteered, but assistance should be given if requested to protect company personnel or property. Company personnel will not sign complaints or warrants for arrest without first obtaining the approval of the director of loss prevention and security.

If unusual circumstances seem to require the presence of an officer of the law, and theft of property is involved, company employees should state the verifiable facts and let the officer make any accusations or arrests. If a breach of the peace or disorderly conduct is involved, every effort should be made to settle it with the offender on a friendly basis and without calling for the assistance of law enforcement agencies.

All necessary arrests should be made by the officers of the law and under no circumstances should company personnel arrest anyone or restrain the liberty of any person unless a crime has actually been committed by that individual in the presence of, and to the positive knowledge of, the company personnel involved, or unless restraint or seizure is necessary for the protection of other employees or becomes necessary to prevent irretrievable loss of property of substantial value.

It should be understood that the detention of employees after their regular hours of duty, for the purpose of questioning by company personnel in connection with any investigation or possible criminal action, may later be construed by the courts as constituting an arrest. Such detention *must not* happen unless (1) the employee is clearly told that he is free to leave at any time after his regular tour of duty if he so desires and (2) nonmanagement personnel will be paid for any time spent in connection with the investigation.

When company property or personal property is known to be missing and there is reason to believe that a specific employee is responsible, direct accusations should not be made by a company official. Neither should the suspect be asked to step into a company office to be questioned. Instead, a security investigator of the company will be called for or, if a security investigator is unavailable and the situation requires it, an officer of the law will be called.

All employees of the company are obliged to place themselves above reproach in implication and in facts relative to misuse or misappropriation of company property and funds. Employees are expected to be ever alert to apparent misuse or misappropriation of company property or money, or to situations or conditions that may result in loss of merchandise or funds. It is the responsibility of the individual employee to immediately report instances of misuse or theft to the appropriate supervisor.

All supervisors are responsible for fully informing their subordinates of security regulations and the resulting consequences of any violation. In addition, all supervisors should immediately inform the security department of facts that indicate the possibility of a company loss. At all times, the director of loss prevention and security has the responsibility for advising the executive vice-president of pertinent investigations or indications of procedural weaknesses within the company systems. The above is in no way intended to preclude the assignment of security investigators to other types of inquiries and investigations, when so directed or requested by appropriate management officials.

A suggested set of company security rules appears in the Appendix.

Employee theft

HUMAN FRAILTIES BEING what they are, it cannot be assumed that employees will be instinctively efficient or completely honest. In most instances, workers do want to be both efficient and honest, and these qualities can be cultivated and maintained through attitudes and controls within the working environment.

Early man got his food, clothing, and shelter wherever he could. He stole from his fellows and hoarded edibles for the future. He seemed to have followed a basic instinct to acquire as a part of his basic instinct for survival. Even today, society frequently, and unfortunately, measures an individual's achievements by the extent of his acquisitions.

In the development of civilization, primitive tribes set up basic rules for the ownership of personal objects, and eventually there was recognition of the right to own flocks and herds and land itself. In time, most individuals came to realize that it is socially destructive to steal the property of another. Nevertheless, man still seems to have a basic instinct to acquire, sometimes controlled by good moral principles and sometimes inclined toward theft. What this means is that honesty may be merely a concept of human intelligence—a personal standard that worked out as man developed religious principles and as society formulated laws for the protection of property. Man's instinct to acquire is not a justification for theft, but may be one of the underlying factors.

SOME OF THE CONSEQUENCES OF THEFT

If a business suffers a theft, the direct financial loss should be obvious. But this may be only one of the consequences, and other problems involved may be even more costly. If the order cannot be filled because merchandise was taken by a thief, a sale may be lost. When customers cannot be satisfied, goodwill may be damaged—the customer may turn to a competitor who always meets his needs. Then too, insurance costs frequently increase as a result of theft. If the items taken are vital to a manufacturing operation, then the whole production line may be hindered.

Some people make regular pronouncements as to the huge sums of money lost each year to employee theft. The figures quoted may be reasonable, but they are estimates at best. Nevertheless, it is certain that these losses are very great. In addition to those incidents that can be substantiated, a number of crimes of this kind go unsuspected.

Management frequently expresses surprise to learn that a trusted employee has been uncovered as a thief. An individual at any level of business may be involved. On the surface, there may be no difference between the persons who steal and the other workers. The trusted individual often has the greatest opportunity to steal, and may be the last to be suspected. For this reason, management needs to apply controls uniformly—to the old employees as well as to the new.

Employee morale problems may also be involved. Some employees may hesitate to work alongside those that they know to be thieves. Management respect also suffers in the eyes of employees if it appears that company officials are either unconcerned or are incapable of handling the problem.

SOME RATIONALIZATIONS

No one can say with certainty why thefts occur. Some feel that most cases of theft involve three elements: opportunity, temptation, and motive. Employees frequently become involved because of imagined grievances against management, because of excessive debts and living beyond their means, because of drug or alcohol addiction, or because of heavy gambling losses.

Some other students of the problem have concluded that there may be three basic conditions involved: (1) the thief's feeling that he has a real need to take the money or merchandise involved; (2) the thief's rationalization that he is justified, that he has been slighted or "cheated" by the company to some extent; and (3) the thief's belief that he can take something without detection.

The thief's belief of his own need

The thief usually feels that he actually needs the money or item that he takes. In the view of the detached outside observer, the thief may not appear to have any need at all, since he may have sufficient financial means. However, the thief may have set requirements for himself that he feels must be satisfied, whether or not he has the income to afford those goals. From an objective point of view, the thief does not really need the money or merchandise, but he has set it up in his own thinking as an absolute necessity. It is seldom in America that an individual must become a thief to prevent starvation. The culprit may associate with individuals who maintain a certain lifestyle, so the thief feels that he has a "need" to live in the same class. If each of these close associates maintains a motor boat, he may feel compelled to acquire similar sports equipment, regardless of his income.

The need may also be a compelling one; for example, to satisfy a drug craving or alcohol addiction.

Revenge

Many dishonest employees have rationalized that they were justified in stealing from the company. An employee may tell himself that he was only taking something to which he was entitled. He may have been passed up for promotion, or he may regard the stolen object as compensation for overtime that he was forced to work without pay. In effect, the employee may say to himself, "The boss didn't treat me fairly, so the company's got this coming!"

Opportunity

If the employee feels that he has the opportunity to take something without much chance of detection, management should reassess the controls that are in effect. Additional positive steps may be warranted.

Opportunities for theft are often overlooked or are deliberately ignored by supervision or management. When this becomes apparent to workers, theft problems can be anticipated.

To illustrate, a customer walked briskly to the rear of a retail store, picked up a low-quality ice chest, and went from aisle to aisle placing items inside the chest. He then lugged the chest to the checkout counter, where his girlfriend was working the cash register. She gave no indication that she was acquainted with the customer and quickly checked to see whether anyone could observe her in the security mirrors. She then rang up the price of the ice chest, ignoring the expensive items that had been placed inside.

Unless someone had observed closely, nothing unusual appeared to have taken place. If management had been watching, it might have been noted that the same young man came through the store at least twice a day, picking up a number of items and placing them inside a large piece of merchandise. He always went to the same cashier, who never rang up more than one item.

Major thefts, the kind that create headlines, occur on a regular basis. But they account for only a part of the business loss.

\ MANAGEMENT ATTITUDES

Management officials should never underestimate their ability to obtain honest performance. There are any number of ways in which employees can be made aware of the value the company places on integrity. Workers usually follow examples, and it is therefore essential that managers and supervisors adhere to all written agreements or verbal promises that have been made to employees or outside individuals. Through the integrity of their own performance, managers can demonstrate that dishonesty will not be countenanced. It is difficult to hide attitudes from employees. A member of the management team who regularly takes a two-and-a-half-hour lunch cannot retain the respect of employees if he disciplines a production worker who exceeds his midday break by ten minutes.

But not only do employees observe management attitudes toward others in the company, they are frequently influenced by the management outlook toward customers. If management doesn't seem to care whether a customer is cheated by a short merchandise count, this same basic attitude may eventually be reflected in employee performance.

The argument is sometimes made that dishonesty is so common in the outside world that it can never be eliminated in business. But the existence of crime does not justify inclusion of theft losses in the costs of doing business. Business is not necessarily saddled with many of the pressures that are faced by society in general. A private company can still be selective, to some extent, as to the individual it places on the payroll. Management can also control the location where the business is conducted and can regulate procedures under which individual employees conduct their duties. As a result, business theft can be influenced to a considerable degree by management decisions.

Buying questionable merchandise

There is good reason to believe that major truck thefts would decline considerably if retail store owners would refuse to buy cigarettes, meat, liquor, clothing, and similar items offered for sale at prices considerably below the market rate. In a great majority of cases this type of bargain is the end result of a major theft. A business that stands for basic honesty should never buy goods that may have a questionable background.

Discharging for theft

It is usually in the best interest of the company for management to take a positive attitude toward employee theft. When an employee is discharged for this kind of activity, an arbitration hearing may be an outgrowth of the incident. In a good number of cases, the discharge may not be upheld by the labor arbitrator if management has been inclined to compromise in theft cases in the past.

In a recent case in Philadelphia, an industrial linen company was aware that its drivers each pocketed the money from one route customer per week. This was an old practice that had gone on for years, to allow each driver to have "lunch money." After a time some of the drivers began to pocket the proceeds from two customers per week, later increasing this to three. Feeling that the situation had gotten out of hand, the company discharged the worst offender.

In the resulting arbitration hearing, the arbitrator ruled that firing was too severe a penalty and altered the punishment to a short suspension without pay. The arbitrator noted that management should not ignore instances of theft until losses become burdensome and then discharge violators at will.

If a company has adopted an easygoing policy in the past, it may be advantageous to begin a change. This can usually be done only by showing in advance that a new policy is in effect. This change must be clearly brought home to the employees, by posting notices on the company bulletin board, by prominent warnings at employee meetings, by statements to this effect in employee pay envelopes, and by other effective means. This may also be the time when union representatives should be informed in writing that management has adopted a change in policy and that discharge will be required in all future cases.

Attempted theft

In the effect on employer-employee relationships, an attempted theft may be just as serious as the act. It is the complete lack of concern for the company's property that makes a thief an undesirable employee, regardless of his failure in completing the crime.

Any employee, or anyone for that matter, has a right to refuse information to police officers, if the information would implicate him in a crime. This right to remain silent is guaranteed under the Fifth Amendment to the Constitution. This does not guarantee the employee the right to continued employment, however. An employee can be fired if he refuses to furnish management with information he possesses that would implicate himself or others in a theft. Arbitrators and the courts usually say that an employer has a right to absolute honesty and cooperation if the employee wishes to avoid discharge.

It should be noted that an employee cannot be prosecuted if he admits theft in exchange for an employer's promise that prosecution will be withheld. In other words management cannot back out on a promise of this nature.

THEFT BY SUPERVISORS

A supervisor may be in a better position to steal than the individual store manager or rank-and-file worker. Usually, employees and managers will not question a direct order given by a supervisor. As a result, the supervisor may have a free hand with considerable amounts of merchandise. In Florida, a member of management discovered that a district supervisor was making fraudulent transfers of groceries from one retail store to another. These groceries never arrived at the designated sore, but went directly to the garage behind the supervisor's country home.

This same grocery chain had discovered a year previously that another district supervisor was stealing merchandise allegedly for transfer to another store and using it to stock a small grocery store a short distance away. Investigation subsequently revealed that the supervisor owned a 50 percent interest in the small retail store where the groceries were eventually sold.

A midwestern meat-packing company experienced regular losses in hams, bacon, and other quality products. Security guards were never able to discover significant breaches of security, and the losses went unexplained for a long time. Eventually, one of the company's outside salesmen discovered that the hams were being offered for sale in a tavern over one hundred miles from the plant. Realizing that the tavern was not a regular customer, management requested a police investigation.

By tracing backward through three sources, it was learned that one of the meat packer's supervisors had managed to get merchandise out on almost any weekend. This had been done through a locked coal chute at the back of the plant production area. The coal chute was padlocked from the inside, and management had always retained good control of the keys to this lock. The code number on the base of the lock was not scratched off, however, and the thief had obtained a duplicate key through an unscrupulous locksmith. This company had not used coal as a source of power for many years, but no one had ever thought of welding the coal chute shut to protect the integrity of the building perimeter. Because of similar cases of this kind, it is suggested that a systematic review be regularly made of the building exits. Regardless of first appearances, any exit is a potential avenue for the removal of stolen property.

THE EARLY-BIRD SYNDROME

There is always a danger of merchandise theft if employees are allowed to work unsupervised. Some members of management find it difficult, especially when good workers are hard to find, to view the early bird as being anything other than an enthusiastic, eager employee. Actual cases indicate that it is relatively easy to steal merchandise 15 or 20 minutes before the arrival of the supervisor or co-workers. For this reason, some companies do not allow employees to punch time cards or to go into production areas more than 10 to 15 minutes before a shift begins.

PACKAGE CONTROLS

Unless package passes are used, typewriters, calculators, and other equipment may be removed from business offices almost at will. Responsibiltiy for package passes should be assigned and enforced without exception by building guards or after-hours elevator operators.

Information on the pass form should completely describe the article by brand, make, color, and serial number if available. The guard or elevator operator should look inside the package, never taking for granted that the package contains only the articles described on the pass.

One of the essential aspects of the control system involves the use of a two-part form. One part should be given to the person carrying the package, and the carbon copy should be retained by the the carbon copy in the supervisor's book. This is to insure that no unsupervisor who authorizes the removal. The passes collected by the guard should be reviewed regularly and a comparison made with authorized additions appear on the original copy of the pass.

If the building has tenants, they should be required to follow the system used by others in the building.

Figure 2 shows a form of this kind.

MARKING COMPANY PROPERTY

There are three basic reasons for marking company property: (1) A thief will often hesitate to steal something if he realizes it can be identified; (2) identification makes it possible for a police agency to locate the owner when stolen property is recovered; and (3) marking also allows property to be positively identified in court.

In recent years many companies have used an electric pencil engraver or electric tool marker to identify property. The superhard tungsten carbide tip of this device makes it useful in etching company identification on almost any material—metal, wood, plastic, or glass. Rather than write out the full name of the company, some businesses etch out symbols or identification numbers. One New Jersey company maintains a national data bank for each identification number in the event it is not readily available through local police sources.

Some companies have found that it pays to paint symbols or attach company markings on all property where these marks can be applied.

If markings are not used, it is suggested that a file be maintained

Figure 2. A package pass.

REMOVAL AUTHORIZATION	No.
	DATE

TO: FREIGHT DOCK CLERK
  or SECURITY GUARDS·

M_____

is authorized to remove from _____ Building on _____

the following articles:_____

_____

_____

_____

TENANT AUTHORIZATION BY	
BUILDING MANAGEMENT AUTHORIZATION BY	COUNTERSIGNATURE

This form should be handed to the clerk or guard checking the articles, who will countersign and return it to the issuing authority.

of the serial numbers of all office machines such as typewriters and calculators and special equipment of every kind. It is often possible to determine the serial number of a missing machine by eliminating all those still on hand from the master inventory list. There is always a good possibility of recovery of a stolen item if the serial number can be furnished to the pawnshop detail of nearby police departments.

An odorless, colorless spray can now be applied to almost any object with a virtually undetectable, permanent mark of ownership. This spray consists of a combination of chemical-trace elements that is almost as individual and definite as a person's fingerprints. About 134 million combinations of the trace chemicals are available. When the chemical combination has been sprayed on an object, a trace of the elements can later be linked to the company that uses this individual spray.

Since this chemical solution is odorless and colorless, it is not apparent that the property has been marked, thus eliminating one of the psychological values of marking. The company selling this solution suggests that use be made of a warning sign to notify everyone that all valuable items on the premises have been marked with a tracing agent for ready identification by the police department.

Losses may occur when production employees on late shifts go into maintenance areas to obtain tools needed to perform some of their duties. Sometimes these employees remove additional tools reserved for the use of maintenance specialists on the day shift. When lack of accountability results from activity of this kind, tool replacement costs are apt to get out of line.

Some managers have solved this problem by furnishing basic tools to production employees on the second and third shifts, holding those individuals responsible for tools issued. It is then possible to impose stringent penalties for breaking into maintenance storage lockers to obtain additional items.

EMPLOYEE "APPROPRIATION" OF SUPPLIES AND EQUIPMENT

Many company articles that employees take home may have little monetary value as individual items, and the company may buy them in hugh quantities. But theft tends to be habit-forming. The employee who appropriates a few blank envelopes to pay his utility bills may thereafter take home a surplus typewriter "to catch up on his personal correspondence." If there is no inquiry about the machine, it may remain at his home indefinitely. It is difficult, of course, to know where to draw the line. But after a time this borrowing for keeps must be regarded as plain dishonesty, regardless of the original intent.

Honest employees frequently know that thefts occur in their departments, but they say nothing to their co-workers who are involved. What they have chosen to ignore is that with rising costs and competition, an accumulation of small thefts can affect the company's profits. Nationally, the loss to employees who take home company items runs into millions of dollars. Employees who ignore this problem are hurting themselves, as at least a part of this money could have gone into employee benefits or higher salaries.

Because of repeated thefts of tools, some companies allow workers to borrow tools with management approval. If employees are required to go past a guard, a package pass may be issued. This is satisfactory in theory, but in actual practice many of these tools are never returned. A Chicago wholesale company handles this problem by preparing an extra copy of the package pass. The extra carbon is routed to a supervisor, who maintains a folder of all tools outstanding on loan. If the item has not been returned within two weeks, the employee's immediate supervisor is instructed to look into the matter.

TRASH DISPOSAL AND THEFT

Trash disposal is one of the problems often closely connected with employee theft. It would be a mistake to simplify retail or wholesale loss problems to those of the trash container alone. But the business-trash area has consistently troubled many kinds of companies.

There are a number of reasons for this. Stolen merchandise can easily be concealed in the trash that is taken out of the building; the thief may reclaim the stolen articles after he has left the premises. The trash bin is often conveniently accessible to the rear door to the building, where activities are seldom observed by management. The company thief usually reasons that if the stolen item should be observed in the trash, managament may believe that it got there through an employee error.

Many retail and wholesale establishments have solved this problem by requiring all trash to be taken out at a specific time, under supervision. Better control can usually be maintained if an outside janitorial firm is not allowed to take out the trash and if janitorial duties are performed during regular business hours rather than during the middle of the night.

Using the trash dumpster as a storage area for stolen items can also be controlled by locking the dumpster after trash has been stored in it. Some trash-removal services do not allow this procedure, however, as they do not want to retain a key to open the dumpster at the time trash is removed.

Another approach is to retain trash receptacles in a locked room for collection and disposal on a weekly basis. This will usually eliminate theft, but may add to the danger of fire. Other companies have adopted the practice of pushing the trash dumpster inside the warehouse at the close of the working day. Thus a dishonest employee is prevented from coming back to retrieve an article secreted in the trash dumpster; however, this situation also increases the possibility of fire losses. It is suggested that a procedure of this kind be followed only with the approval of the company's fire insurance agent.

The possibility of concealing stolen items may also be reduced by the use of a trash compactor. But unless access is carefully controlled to the compactor, it is always a possibility for a neighborhood child to get into the machine and be injured or killed.

RESPECTING EMPLOYEE CONFIDENCES

Loyal employees will often advise supervisors or managers about specific theft problems, provided that they respect management. If management seems unavailable or unsympathetic to employee concerns, then little feedback can be anticipated.

It is basic that the confidence of loyal employees should be protected under all circumstances.

JANITORIAL SERVICES

Employees of many janitorial services are bonded in order to protect their clients. It is not often, however, that this is of much value to business. Theft by a janitorial employee must be proved to the bonding company, beyond question, before the bonding company will pay the claim. Even if a claim is honored, it is seldom possible to make any recovery of the time lost for processing, prosecution, and other aspects of the claim.

When possible, janitorial services should be performed during hours of operation, or at least partial operation, of the business so that supervision will be available at all times. Further, this system does away with the need to issue keys to the janitorial service.

When the cleaning must be performed at night, the janitor should have only the keys to the office area, and should not be able to gain access to the warehouse or stockrooms.

Similarly, the janitor should not be allowed to clean the company computer center unsupervised. There is too much concentration of sensitive and costly equipment and tapes or disks there. Essential materials could be mistakenly removed, or the janitor could accidentally activate a machine and destroy sensitive information.

SALVAGE OR SCRAP ACCUMULATION

Management must control the total processes of the business. This includes side products that may result, or salvage items that may be worth a great deal. It is taken for granted that a metals manufacturing company or a machine shop will exercise controls to accumulate scrap brass, aluminum, and other metal salvage. Some other businesses do not always seem alert to the possibilities for additional income for salvage and may lose considerable revenue.

For many years some industrial laundries and uniform rental concerns allowed employees to sell scrap rags out the back door of the plant, with no accounting to management. Some of these companies found that the employees were accepting the weight tickets of unscrupulous rag dealers, who were not weighing the bags. In many instances the dealers were not paying for the full amount.

Even after proper procedures have been set up for the accumulation and sale of rags, experience shows that regular audits must be made to remind employees not to throw scrap into trash bins.

If employees are allowed to carry away salvageable items, there is always a possibility that regular merchandise may be deliberately damaged. A large hospital in California allowed a technician to remove old X-ray plates from the silver that could be salvaged from them. The business manager of the hospital was shocked to learn later that the technician was removing some X-rays before the end of the seven-year retention period required by state law.

A Philadelphia manufacturer of flour mixes was also shocked to discover that one of his foremen occasionally made an error that spoiled a whole batch of mix and sold that batch to a poultry feed company for personal gain.

In cutting and packaging meats, a supermarket or grocery may accumulate considerable quantities of bone, fat, and scrap. There is a ready market for these byproducts. Here, too, it is recommended that weight tickets be prepared on the premises, with a supervisor observing the transaction and an independent witness for each ticket.

Payments for scrap or salvage should never be given to employees but should be made by check payable to the front office of the business. There should also be a reconciliation between all salvage tickets and the payments made by salvage companies.

Quality control inspectors for a New Jersey manufacturer of plastic garden hoses rejects about one percent of the hoses formed in the manufacturing process. A technique used at a companion plant in New York state makes it possible to convert these salvaged plastic hose sections into reusable plastic pellets.

With warehouse space at a premium, the New Jersey plant followed the practice of piling rejected hoses in a vacant section of the employee parking lot. Brass couplings had not been attached to these hose sections, and the salvage appeared to have no real value to anyone in the neighborhood.

The New Jersey plant remained open on a three-shift basis, twenty-four hours a day, five days a week. There was no guard service, and the plant was empty on weekends. A cruising police car observed a truck on the company parking lot on a Sunday afternoon. Investigation subsequently disclosed that a local trucker had been picking up about half of the salvaged hose output for many months. He had been unable to sell the salvaged plastic locally, but had found a ready market about 75 miles away.

If scrap can be classified into different grades of materials, it is recommended that it be separated so as to get the highest prices available.

Where logical to do so, it is also suggested that scrap barrels or containers be locked, as experience shows that a few employees may carry off items such as brass and copper scraps on a regular basis.

PART
3

OFFICE PROBLEMS

Protecting company records and computer data

SOME PEOPLE IN MANAGEMENT feel that information is the one indispensable element and that the company could not function without it. Other executives pay only lip service to records management. But in almost any given year, reliable records maintained by fire insurance companies indicate that approximately half the companies that lose records on account of fire or other disaster are never able to reopen for business.

Because of this potential danger, it is suggested that a vital records protection plan be set up. It should begin with an assessment as to just which records are essential. As a practical matter, experts on records management sometimes state that no more than 2 percent of a company's records are vital. This figure increases somewhat for banks or financial institutions, but it does not mean that the bulk of company records are absolutely necessary.

Records management involves control over the creation, processing, filing, or storage and retrieval of company information. Management should continue these functions as long as the records have value. When records are of no further use to a company, they should be put through a disposal process. A good system must protect or back up those documents regarded as vital to the organization, its stockholders, customers, and employees.

RESPONSIBILITY FOR COMPUTER SECURITY

In the present-day world of the computer, most business records are concentrated on computer tapes or disks. Damage to the computer or its records could cripple an entire organization. It is therefore axiomatic that good protection should be given to the computer and computer software.

Joint efforts are required

A program that has the objective of preventing loss of computer records must combine the abilities of management, the director of loss prevention and security, and the company's data processing officials and employees.

Most companies have learned that it is helpful to have a clearly formulated set of procedural rules, with designated responsibility for handling specific aspects of the program. Unless company officials insist on periodic audits and reviews of procedures, it is doubtful that compliance with established regulations will be effective. The director of data processing, as well as the director of loss prevention and security, must call attention to the security vulnerabilities that arise from time to time and must implement recommendations to correct these hazards.

Total security, of course, is only an ideal. Costs and operating problems increase as this goal is approached. But if the essential business records are concentrated in the computer system, then there must be a compromise between costs and objectives.

To provide protection of records, a program must bring a welding of interlocking components. At the minimum these should include:

Physical protection
Procedural safeguards
Processing restrictions that regulate software access
EDP personnel selection
Audit controls and insurance protection

Location of the physical facility

Crimes and social problems seem to occur far more in some neighborhoods than in others. Management should therefore choose a site away from a high-crime area. Ideally, the computer should be housed in an area where programmers, operators, and other employees feel safe in coming to work on night shifts.

Then, too, if key records and costly equipment are housed in a well-constructed building, there is a good probability that most physical catastrophies can be eliminated. These are the typical problems caused by tornadoes, hurricanes, overflowing rivers, or bursting water mains in the structure.

Loss from fire is perhaps the most serious environmental hazard to guard against in most locations. This aspect of computer protection is both complex and technical, and may require the assistance of outside experts. A good program for the inspection of fire-fighting equipment should be set up, and employees should be indoctrinated in verifying the workability and use of the fire-detection and -suppressant systems that are installed.

Access to the installation

It is important that access to the computer installation and sensitive areas be physically controlled. Physical security consultants should be utilized to recommend door-locking and -access systems, alarms, guard protection, and adequate perimeter controls through the use of locks, fencing, night lighting, and other techniques and devices.

Unless an adequate survey of the facility is made, it will often be found that access can be obtained through unprotected doors, windows, dumbwaiter shafts, vent openings, trash chutes, or crawl space in the false ceiling or underfloor areas.

After a physical survey has been made, however, it will be useless unless employees respect and utilize the controls and devices. After a time, even conscientious employees tend to overlook the basic security requirements. Accordingly, it is necessary for management to make regular inspections to verify that systems are not being circumvented because of carelessness or lack of interest.

BACKUP SYSTEMS

The computer installation may suffer serious loss unless provision is made for three kinds of backup systems:

1. The computer itself may fail mechanically, and a backup processor may be needed. While most computers are highly reliable, any kind of machinery may encounter problems. Few companies can afford a spare computer. It is suggested that the director of data processing locate an outside computer that can be utilized in the event of a breakdown. One of the problems here is that changes may be made

from time to time in the peripheral hardware that is used with the computer processor. When an emergency arises it may then be found that the outside system is no longer compatible with the system that it is expected to back up. Then, too, an outside company that has promised to make computer time available may find that usage has increased, so that no free time is left. It is therefore advisable to make regular tests of outside machinery, as well as to verify that it continues to be available.

2. Backup electric power may be advisable. With increasing power demands throughout the United States, there is a possibility that power production could be curtailed for extended periods. A backup generator, such as a diesel oil-burning system, may be advisable. Storage of an adequate supply of fuel is also a requirement in providing backup capability of this kind.

3. Computers generate a considerable amount of heat. Air conditioning is essential for the maintenance of operating temperatures in many locations, so failure will close down the computer. A second, completely independent system may be necessary to back up the air-conditioning installation. If both systems are dependent on a single electric power source, then the backup air-conditioning unit may be useless.

Backup tapes or disks

One of the basic concerns of computer security is to have access to backup tapes or disks. By retaining operating systems software backup, along with a prior generation of the computer tapes, it should be possible to add current transactions and reconstruct the business records.

It is vital, however, that the backup tapes (or disks) be kept at another location so that they would not also be destroyed in the event of a fire or physical disaster at the computer location. It may also be desirable to set up clearly written retention instructions pertaining to all vital records, including directions for the implementation of these instructions.

Frequently employees fail to remove backup tapes from the computer facility unless management has a regular program for auditing the outside storage procedures. It is also important to make certain that a saboteur or disgruntled employee does not have access to either the primary tapes or the backup versions; they should be kept locked at an off-site location.

Emergency plans

From a practical standpoint, it may be advisable to work out an emergency shutdown program, as well as a plan for recovery. These plans should vary with the needs of the individual installation.

If the plans are to be workable, individual employee duties and administrative responsibility should be spelled out in advance, explained to those involved, and reduced to writing. Experience shows that employees should act out their individual roles in such a plan, so that there would be a minimum of confusion if an actual emergency should arise.

Addresses and telephone numbers of computer department employees should, if possible, be available at a duplicate location.

OPERATING PRECAUTIONS

If it is possible for a programmer to run his own programs without supervision, then he may be involved in fraud against his employer. He could, for example, instruct the computer to make an embezzlement, and he could subsequently erase the instructions, leaving no observable trace of the transaction. For this reason, there should be a basic physical separation between programmers and operators. It is advisable that master file changes originate in the individual departments of the business, with close supervision to insure that unauthorized modifications are not made by EDP personnel.

Supervision should retain operating programs under lock and key. Definite procedures should be set up and verified by auditing to make sure that programs are not modified, documented, or used without authority.

Other controls may also be helpful from an operational standpoint. It is suggested that a log be kept, specifying the cause of each machine halt, along with the corrective action that was taken. This kind of record may be used to eliminate future breakdowns, if adequately reviewed and evaluated by supervising management.

Controlling the tape library

An adequate control system should be worked out to fix responsibility for the possession and utilization of all tapes or disks in the tape library. The charge-out system for usage and return should be audited, with an immediate investigation undertaken in the event that any records should be unaccounted for.

It is also proper to audit all times used on the computer, as it has sometimes been found that employees may operate a private business on the company computer unless this verification is made.

Disposing of computer records

When confidential business records are no longer needed, it may be advisable to destroy them. Due caution should be exercised to make certain that burning, shredding, or mutilation actually takes place. Unless proper precautions are taken, defective tapes containing readable information may become available to unauthorized persons. Companies that sell punch cards for paper salvage should make certain that they are scrambled or mutilated prior to sale.

Employee security

It has been asserted that beneath the surface of every business employee lies a possible security hazard. If management knew where to look for the conditions that cause problems of this kind, preventive action could be taken. At any rate, as mentioned, persons of questionable reliability should not be hired. And after employees are placed on the job, they should be told that management relies on them to protect the integrity of the computer installation. They should be aware that the company appreciates them and that they are part of the team. If shown respect, employees can be expected to look out for the company's interests.

Employee vigilance

Employees should understand the hazards that go along with tours of the computer site. Even with an alert escort, a curious person may carry off a souvenir or unintentionally cause damage. It is preferable for management to discontinue all tours, but vigilant employees can help avoid problems if the company insists on allowing visitors.

Employees should also be briefed as to their responsibilities to keep out disgruntled former employees, friends of employees, or anyone else who does not have clearance.

Protecting
business secrets

ALMOST EVERY COMPANY would like to know what its competition is doing. The desired information frequently centers around commercial secrets: chemical formulas, manufacturing techniques, scheduling, customer lists, product designs, and expansion plans. Practically every company has confidential information of some kind.

In attempting to learn the secrets of their competition, some companies engage in industrial espionage. Management officials sometimes try to explain away their participation in this activity as just another type of marketing research. They reason that other companies are just as active in attempting to ferret out secrets.

The real extent of this kind of dishonest and criminal activity can only be estimated. From time to time feature stories in the newspapers carry headlines such as: "Secrets for Sale: Industrial Spying," "Six Billion Dollar Drain on U.S. Business by Espionage," and "Spies, Counterspies Ply Trade in Business World."

According to such accounts, both professional agents and amateur spies steal an estimated $6 billion a year in information, ideas, and experimental devices and materials from American companies. These news accounts usually imply that this activity is becoming even more widespread. The estimated $6 billion loss may represent an accurate figure, but this is only an estimate at best. In addition, some of the news accounts may be exaggerated considerably. It is to be noted, however, that a considerable amount of this kind of activity can be substantiated, so the possibilities for business loss should not be discounted. Many companies may be susceptible to loss, either from their own employees selling secrets or from extraneous penetration.

WHAT IS A TRADE SECRET?

Generally, a trade secret is a process or a formula, not patented, and guarded within the knowledge of persons using it, to prepare merchandise or articles for trade with a commercial value. A trade secret is a business device, mechanism, process, tool, or chemical compound known only to the proprietor of the business and those employees to whom it is necessary to reveal it. It is a device or a process used regularly in the operation of a business.

PROTECTION UNDER EXISTING LAWS

There is only a small body of law that applies to industrial espionage. The problem has been recognized for a number of years, but it is a new, unsettled area in which few cases have actually been tried in the courts.

In most cases of theft of business information, the rightful owner is still in possession of his or her confidential material. What happened is that the secret was copied and that person no longer has sole possession. The owner can still use it, but so can everyone else. The owner may have been injured just as surely as if the secret had been completely lost to him.

Federal and state laws that prohibit theft or embezzlement of property had their origin in the ancient English common law, long before the development of the industrial revolution. Under the requirements of theft and embezzlement laws, it is necessary for the guilty party to physically take the stolen or embezzled property and carry it away. In industrial espionage, the property in question may never be removed from the company premises. Only a copy of a document or a secret formula may have been taken. In addition, another requirement of the ancient criminal laws made it necessary for the owner of the stolen property to have been deprived of the use or possession of the property involved before it could be regarded as stolen.

Recently, there has been increased realization in the courts that duplication of intellectual property or trade secrets may be as damaging to the owner as loss of money or merchandise. In most states, the courts now recognize the right of a business to protect information such as marketing data, proposed expansion plans, shop and industrial techniques, new product information, and customer lists.

It is not always necessary to business success to protect secret information indefinitely. Frequently it is only a question of time until secret chemical formulas or mechanical techniques can be duplicated by competition. This has been more apparent in recent years owing to the increased use of research and development engineers and scientists.

If the new product catches the fancy of the public, the available market may be monopolized within a short time. Protection of the new product or the processes used to produce it may be necessary only during this lead time. Therefore, the concentration should be on protecting the secret long enough to enable the new product to capture the market.

LEGAL ACTION

There are three basic types of legal action a company may use against individuals or other companies that steal business secrets.

1. A lawsuit for money damages can be filed against the ex-employee or spy who is responsible for stealing the business secret. In actual practice, the person taking information frequently does not have a great deal of money to repay the company losing the trade secret.

2. A lawsuit for money damages can be filed against the company that bought the trade secret or wrongfully made use of it. The injured company can obtain an accounting for all profits made by the illegal use and can obtain money damages to repay for its loss of profits.

3. An injunction can be obtained from the court. This is a legal process that forbids the defecting employee, industrial spy, or the business wrongfully using the trade secret from making further use of it. Violation of the injunction can result in the offender being placed in contempt of court and jailed until the contempt is removed by compliance with the court's injunction.

COMBATING INDUSTRIAL ESPIONAGE

It is suggested that management should consider the problem of industrial espionage from three points of view:

1. What information should the employee be allowed to reveal in technical meetings, conferences, and the like?
2. What can management do to protect against willful dishonesty?
3. What company information can the employee take with him when he changes to another job?

Information revealed by honest employees. Businesses are frequently surprised to learn how much information is divulged in an effort to prove company expertise to competitive companies. Usually this is a well-intended effort on the part of employees to maintain an impression of superiority with regard to a business rival or competitor.

An approach that can be taken here is to completely isolate employees from all outside scientific and professional contacts. This is an extreme view, and usually only succeeds in completely discouraging employee creativity. This, of course, is not a desirable result because every company needs accomplishment and creativity from its employees.

At the other extreme, a company that declines to furnish scientific and engineering personnel with some guidelines may find that these employees disclose far more than the company intended. As previously indicated, many of these disclosures may be made for the purpose of impressing contemporaries in other companies.

It is suggested that management strike a compromise, not seeking to muzzle employees completely, but holding briefing sessions as to what can be revealed without serious damage to the company's position in the marketplace.

Preventing employees from taking confidential material. The courts have consistently taken the attitude that they will not protect a company's trade secrets unless the company is willing to protect itself in a reasonable fashion. Before awarding money damages or prohibiting a competitor from using stolen material or information, the courts usually require the following action by the company that complains of the loss of trade secrets:

1. There must be a showing that the trade secret was something regarded as of unusual worth to the owner. A mere showing that the owner regards all his records as valuable is not sufficient.

2. There must be a showing that the individual who stole the information or technical process was aware of the value of the trade secret and that the thief's activities reflected this same attitude.

3. There must be a showing that the thief's activities violated the relationship of trust that existed and that he used the information in a conspiracy or benefited by sale of the information.

In actual practice it may be almost impossible for a business to satisfy all three requirements.

Conflict between employee and business interests. The courts usually express the attitude that new industrial techniques or newly invented products work to the benefit of the community in general. On the other hand, if a commercial organization cannot obtain profits as a result of research and development, then there will be little advantage in maintaining scientific or experimental programs for the development of new products. Some protection must be given to the intellectual property of the company that develops it.

In many instances there may be a conflict as to whether the individual worker has a right to the device or idea he develops or whether it belongs to the company that employs him. If an employee obtains a new job, he still retains his intellectual capacity, which is a composite of his experiences for his prior employer, the knowledge obtained from fellow workers, his individual intellectual ability, and his own experimental information.

Since the interests of the employee and the company are often in conflict, the courts usually say that they will not limit a person's right to make a living. This does not mean, however, that the individual can disclose secret formulas or processes developed by him or her while working for a company.

Noncompete agreements

Some companies protect their trade secrets by signing "noncompete" agreements with employees. Usually, these contracts either forbid unauthorized revelation of trade secrets or they limit future activities that may be in conflict with those of the company. The right of an individual worker to continue to make a living, as previously noted, is respected by the courts. But if the individual is the proprietor of a business and signs an agreement not to compete in future years, the facts are viewed differently by the courts. In cases of this kind, the courts will generally issue an injunction forbidding the competition. If the individual is competing at some distance from the territory covered by the company, the courts will usually say that a noncompete agreement will not be upheld because the company is not conducting business in that geographical area anyway.

Employee concern for trade secrets

It is usually in the best interest of the company to make employees aware of the problems involved in protecting trade secrets. It is helpful to let individual workers know that this protection is necessary to a profitable operation and that everyone in the company should benefit by this program.

This does not mean that management should disclose confidential information to anyone and everyone. Decisions should be made at the outset as to which employees will be allowed to work with secret information or confidential processes. Such disclosure should be made on a need-to-know basis. If management spells out the problems and responsibilities here, employees will usually perform up to expectations.

Physical protective devices

Management should continue to use whatever physical protective devices may seem logical. These should include such basic requirements as physically verifying the use of safes, locking cabinets, office door locks, and protective devices on windows. Access to critical areas of the building should be closely controlled, and receptionists or guards should regulate the movement of unauthorized persons.

Destroying secret documents

When there is no longer any need to maintain secret information, steps should be taken to dispose of this material. Since incinerators are prohibited in most large cities or industrial areas, many companies have made use of paper shredders to destroy secret material. If there is still a question as to the value of the material, it is suggested that it be shredded.

Control of duplicating processes

Some companies take extraordinary steps to protect their confidential materials, but have no restriction on duplicating secrets. If copies are made, it is suggested that they be collected under the same standards that are used to protect the original material.

Classifying documents

One method for impressing employees with the confidential nature of information is to classify the material as "secret" or "confidential." Other companies frequently mark confidential documents with a stamp, pointing out that the document is the exclusive property of the company and is not to be carried away or reproduced without authorization.

One of the first places that any commercial spy will search is the executive's wastebasket. There he may find material that may be of benefit to a competitor. By checking for only a few days, a great deal may be learned about the executive's habits and interests, on and off the job. The variety of information in the wastebasket may include the company's future plans, trade secrets, a patentable process, and other valuable information.

If there is a considerable volume of classified papers, the company may consider using a logbook or charge-out register to maintain accountability for individual papers. If the volume of these documents is sufficient to warrant a librarian, a full or part-time librarian may be needed to properly maintain custody and accountability of confidential papers.

Techniques of industrial spies

Persons who steal industrial secrets may utilize a number of secret techniques. Hidden microphones may be used to pick up conversations in company offices or telephone lines may be tapped.

Some magazine and newspaper stories give the impression that illegal microphones and telephone taps are used very frequently. No one, of course, knows the full extent to which these techniques are utilized by private investigators or company employees involved in industrial espionage. Because these installations require a trespass, and subject the violator to possible criminal prosecution, it is likely that telephone taps and microphone installations may be far less common than is sometimes supposed.

If there is reason to believe that a company telephone has been tapped or that a microphone has been planted in a business conference room, it is recommended that help be obtained from an electronics expert. Installations of this kind can be detected by making "sweeps" or by other scientific techniques. There are a number of so-called experts in this field who do not have the proper training to make investigations of this kind and it is suggested that technical assistance of this kind not be requested unless the reputation of the firm has been previously established.

Exit interviews

Many employees who leave the company are not in a position to reveal company secrets. If the departing employee is in possession of sensitive information, it is suggested that he be afforded an exit interview immediately prior to leaving the company. It is recommended that this interview be conducted in an open, frank manner and that the interviewing official solicit suggestions and honest criticism that may help the company in future dealings with employees.

It should be pointed out that every individual must be concerned about his own objectives and future accomplishments and that the company wishes him well in this regard. At the same time, it should be tactfully pointed out that the departing employee is in possession of trade secrets and that it is to the company's interest to verify that he has turned in all confidential materials, specifications, manuals, notebooks, company keys, and property. In addition, he should be tactfully put on notice that company secrets must remain with the company and that as an honorable person, the departing employee is expected to abide by this commitment.

Some companies that are involved in secret projects and experimentation have been successful in appealing to departing employees to sign a termination agreement. In presenting this written agreement for signature, the interviewing official usually appeals to the basic sense of fairness and integrity in the employee. In a high percentage of cases, the departing employee will sign a pledge agreeing to make no disclosures of confidential information to anyone. A document of this kind usually serves as a strong psychological deterrent and may be used as the basis for a lawsuit in some instances where the agreement is violated by the departing employee.

Protecting office buildings

IT IS OFTEN IMPLIED that present-day crime is restricted to street locations or public areas. The fact is that violence and criminal acts that were once common in beer parlors, dimly lit alleys, small retail stores, and public parks are now taking place in the nation's office buildings at a startling rate. Even high-rise buildings and the executive suite may be involved. In the larger cities, purse snatchings and muggings occur in corridors, elevators, or stairwells of plush buildings so often that taken individually they attract little attention.

Big business organizations have been the target of bombings, both inside and outside the building, since anti-Vietnam war protesters became active. These attacks and bomb threats did bring management to a realization of other problems. A number of companies discovered that drifters came into the building at will, secreting themselves in men's rest rooms until 5 P.M. Then these intruders pilfered whatever they could find in the offices and found their way out of the building without being challenged.

Crime statistics are not reported exclusively on the basis of business location, but the problem has been growing so serious that some companies have relocated in less-populous areas. Even in outlying areas, however, it has often been found that company offices are not immune from criminal acts.

Regardless of location, there are a number of reasons why business offices are vulnerable. In the first place, almost any large building is required to have a number of entrances to provide sufficient exits in case of fire.

Then, too, a necessary part of business may involve the frequent entry and departure of deliverymen, maintenance employees, and after-hours customers and messengers. Employees are usually hesitant about challenging strangers, and there is a sense of anonymity in large structures.

Much of the problem may be centered around multi-tenant buildings, where the unknown person in the corridor is presumed to have business with one of the other tenants. Of course the problem could be solved by escorting everyone, but in many locations the cost would be prohibitive, and the tenants may move out if they feel that security interferes with job performance.

Some of the blame for this problem may be attributed to the increase in drug usage, with addicts searching the building for anything that can be carried away to be sold or pawned.

Typewriters and office machines, especially pocket calculators, are often taken, along with personal cameras, portable TV sets, coats, and sweaters. If the employee does not really need a pocket calculator, it should not be provided. There are a number of protective devices on the market that are quite effective in preventing typewriters and expensive machines from being carried away. One of the problems here, however, is that most of these devices permanently lock the machine to a desk or table, preventing it from being moved about for the convenience of the employees.

A typical device uses a high-density pressure-sensitive foam tape to secure a base pad. A machine is bolted to an aluminum platform, which is then locked to the base pad by two key locks. Some companies have tried to improve mobility of these locked machines by securing them to wheeled typewriter stands or tables, but this does not prevent the entire stand from being wheeled away. In addition, employee efficiency may be impaired by the inability to move adding machines, typewriters, and other equipment

PERSONAL LOSSES

It is the employee, rather than the company, that sustains loss when a purse or wallet is stolen. Nevertheless, an incident of this kind is damaging to employee morale. Usually the victim is a female secretary or clerical employee who has left her purse unattended when she takes dictation from a company official or goes to the ladies' rest room. The cash loss in such an incident is usually small, but the victim generally is an employee in a low-pay bracket. Over and above the cash loss, additional problems may be anticipated unless credit card companies are promptly notified and unless locks are changed on the victim's apartment or home-entry door.

Management can caution employees to lock up valuables, but some workers are not provided separate desks or lockable facilities, and this is always a time-consuming precaution. Office-access controls may be helpful here, as in other situations. Ideally, all visitors and outside persons should be cleared through a central reception desk. Control can usually be maintained by requiring the receptionist to call the person to be visited and by making that employee responsible for the activities and eventual departure of the outside person. In a system of this kind, it may be advisable to provide the central receptionist with an alarm button that can be used to request assistance from an official or from the company security office. The effectiveness of this system depends on having locks on all office doors opening into public corridors in the building and on keeping those doors locked at all times.

LOBBY AND STAIRWELL CONTROLS

A major bank in the New York City area occupies 5 stories of a high-rise building, leasing out space in 45 additional stories. After a program for lobby control was begun in the building, it was found that security problems were about 15 percent of those reported in the prior year.

Some of the floors of this building are open to the public during daytime hours. Visitors to other floors are required to go through a security receptionist, who calls for verification from the individual to be visited. A pass is then issued, which is worn on the clothing of the visitor and returned at the end of the visit. The pass is color-coded, and the color changed daily. It is good only for the date of issue.

At closing time a guard makes a sweep through each floor of the building to verify that persons staying late are actually employees of the offices in question.

Visitors and employees leaving or entering the building after hours are required to identify themselves to the guard on duty, and are then signed in on a register. As a further precaution, a camera is used to facilitate identification and rapid movement.

The fire code in this area prohibits the use of locking devices on the doors. Access through the stairwells would therefore appear to be quite easy, but pressure mats under the carpeting, photoelectric cells, and stair-stress alarm are strategically placed to alert the guard force of an unauthorized penetration. An alarm, of course, cannot of itself apprehend or detain a wrongdoer. But it allows a small number of guards to control a number of entryways or stairwells.

BUSINESS VAULTS

Many managements use vaults in the company offices for currency, securities, negotiables, and records. Although many of these vaults were built long ago, company officials seldom question whether these vaults really afford much protection against fire, theft, or robbery. The steel door may seem impressive and may itself carry a fire rating. But examination of the ceiling and walls may reveal that the ceiling is of corrugated metal and that the walls afford little fire protection. If specific questions are asked, management may find that the combination to the vault has not been changed for many years.

Frequently it will be discovered that there is a crawl space above the vault ceiling, and a burglar may be able to work for several hours while breaking through the roof of the vault without being observed by police patrols.

If the vault is intended to protect large amounts of currency or negotiables, it is suggested that a determination be made as to whether it has been constructed to vault specifications.

If essential computer tapes or disks are stored in an area of this kind, it is recommended that an expert opinion be obtained as to whether the vault affords adequate fire protection.

MAILROOM LOSSES

Every company should maintain controls over the scales and metering parts of a postal system If a scale is out of balance, excess postal charges may accumulate or letters may reach their destination marked "postage due." This would not result in direct losses, but could prove very damaging to the company's image.

In some companies employees send their personal packages and mail through the company mailroom, especially during the holiday seasons. Spot checks by management may determine whether this is happening. It is not unusual to find that employees have never actually been informed that company facilities may not be used. To prevent unauthorized posting by employees or cleaning personnel after working hours, the heads on postage meters should be locked every night.

Although a company may have a rule against posting personal mail, managers themselves are sometimes guilty of breaking the rule. Mailroom employees may allow this as a favor to management. If the company policy is to be effective, however, it must be applied to top management as well as to all other employees. If there is a likelihood of misuse here, it is suggested that unannounced, random inspection of outgoing mail bags be made.

To prevent loss, non-mailroom employees should not be given access to the mailroom. Any mail or packages that have been left in the mailroom should be locked up overnight, and transactions with the mailroom should be conducted by restricting other employees with a counter or grill-covered window.

If experience proves that an excessive number of packages are lost or damaged in the mail, management should consider using the services of an alternate carrier such as United Parcel Service.

Losses may occur in the postal system itself if the address label indicates that there may be valuables in the package. Postal employees sometimes carry preaddressed labels in their pockets and apply one of them over the legitimate label. The substituted label bears the address of an accomplice or close friend. A method used to avoid such loss is to use a plain label and a return address that do not identify the shipper as a manufacturer of valuables.

Losses from unauthorized telephone calls can usually be eliminated by spot checking a reasonable percentage of the calls or by auditing the entire bill. The latter procedure is preferable. Divisions or sections of a large company can maintain a log at a switchboard or wherever calls are placed. A brief investigation of unlogged calls on the bill will usually show who placed them. A simple form for listing calls on a day-to-day basis is shown in Figure 3.

PETTY CASH

Losses of petty cash may seem of little consequence in many businesses. If continued, however, these losses could be of real concern.

Then, too, some authorities on business embezzlement state that employee dishonesty frequently begins with the petty cash. Account-

Figure 3. Telephone log for auditing calls.

| Division or Company Office: _____ | | | | | | | |
| Dates Covered: _____ | | | | | | | |
Date	Origin	Extension (Caller)	Number & Place Called	Person Called	Reason for Call	Billable (Yes or No) File No.	Time and Charges

ability for all money transactions, large or small, is a basic requirement of loss control.

Accountability should begin with the establishment of a specific fund administered by a specific office employee. To handle needs that will arise when the designated employee is absent, accountability should be continued through an alternate petty cash clerk.

As a practical matter, the petty cash fund should be large enough to handle day-to-day needs without tempting an armed robber or professional burglar.

It is recommended that money never be disbursed from this fund without a corresponding voucher, prepared immediately upon payment. Before money is paid out, it is suggested that the voucher be approved by a designated company official and the receipt portion of the voucher be signed by the person receiving the funds.

It is not unusual to observe vouchers that have been raised in amount, although this can be forestalled by using permanent ink in voucher preparation. It is recommended that the amount of money paid be written out in full, for example "Twenty Dollars," rather than "$20.00" (see Figure 4).

A recommended practice is for the petty cash fund to be replenished by preparing a check in the total amount of all the paid vouchers that have been handled. Many companies follow the practice

Figure 4. A satisfactory petty cash voucher.

```
┌─────────────────────────────────────────────────────────────┐
│  ┌───────────────┐                              ┌──────────┐  │
│  │   ENTERED     │     Petty Cash Voucher       │ No.      │  │
│  └───────────────┘                              └──────────┘  │
│                                                               │
│                                      Date_____    │
│                                                               │
│  PAY TO.....................................  $ 4.39 ........  │
│                                                               │
│      Four and  — — — — — — — — — — — — — —39  Dollar:         │
│  ......................................................       │
│                                                  100          │
│  Expended For..............................................   │
│                                                               │
│  ..........................................................   │
│                                                               │
│  Charge To..................... Account No. ..............    │
│  ───────────────────────────────────────────────────────     │
│  APPROVED BY            │    RECEIVED PAYMENT                  │
│                         │                                      │
└─────────────────────────────────────────────────────────────┘
```

of entering in the general ledger the amount of money in the petty cash fund.

It is also recommended that a responsible member of management examine each voucher on an individual basis, looking for indications of fraud or alteration. After this inspection has been made, the vouchers should be canceled so that they cannot be submitted a second time. A perforating device is helpful here. Some companies use a rubber stamp with ink that cannot be easily erased. In any event, the cancellation should be made through the middle of the voucher so that the cancellation cannot be trimmed off and the voucher be used again.

Approved accounting controls require unannounced audits of vouchers in the petty cash fund, with the account balanced at frequent intervals. This will usually prevent embezzlement or borrowing.

OFFICE SUPPLIES AND EQUIPMENT

Pilfered office supplies and equipment can add considerably to the cost of doing business. Here again, employee attitudes can be cultivated by appealing to the inherent honesty of office personnel.

The principal of an elementary school in Arizona recently received a call from the father of a first-grade student, expressing outrage that the school staff had allowed a classmate of the son to steal his pencil.

"The point is," insisted the father, "that the school is negligent to allow such a thing. The pencil itself is unimportant. I can always get a gross from my office."

Attitudes of this kind compound the problems of waste and pilferage.

Although there is no uniformity in procedures that businesses follow in controlling supplies, individual companies have found the following systems to be helpful.

Some companies maintain office supplies in locked cabinets located in a central storeroom. Rules allow department and staff secretaries to requisition needed items once a week. This allows a supervisor to briefly review requests, department by department, to make sure that the items requested are reasonable.

This approach does away with the problems that result when everyone in the office is allowed to have access to supplies. Knowledgeable persons in the field of employee embezzlement generally agree that opportunity is one of the principal factors in this kind of loss.

Another system that has been found successful is to permit each employee to request needed supplies on a requisition form at a specific time each day. Supervisory approval is not needed in this system, as the quantities requisitioned by each individual will be on file. Management should periodically verify usage to learn whether requests exceed individual needs.

TIME CARDS

Time cards are a valuable tool in controlling a large number of employees. Properly used, they verify employee attendance as well as the accuracy of company payroll records. It is recommended that occasionally management make a check of time cards, choosing 10 to 15 cards at random and physically verifying that an employee by that name is actually at work or is accounted for. An audit of this kind should be made without prior notification to anyone.

After this verification, management should make no effort to conceal the reason for this inquiry. Management has a legitimate right to check production or attendance records anytime, and need make no apology. This practice serves to let employees know that punching a time card for another employee is a serious matter; most companies have a strict rule to the effect that doing so is a dischargeable offense.

It is also suggested that a supervisor initial every error on a time card, in ink. If an employee is actually at work but forgets to punch in, a written notation to that effect should be made by the supervisor or lead man in charge. If such a notation is made as soon as the error is discovered, the possibility for inaccuracy will be considerably reduced.

It is suggested that management make spot checks immediately following a shift break to verify that the time card racks contain no leftover cards, except those of employees who are scheduled to work the next shift.

Overtime pay may create serious loss problems in some companies, since there may be some question as to whether the overtime was authorized. A notation by a supervisor on the individual worker's card, made on a shift-by-shift basis, will usually dispel doubt.

PAYROLL CHECKS

If management is not acquainted with each employee, there is a possibility that a fictitious name can be placed on the payroll. Some companies solve this problem by having one employee draw up payroll records and a second employee in the accounting office make an independent verification by a compilation from employee time cards.

To make certain that there are no "ghosts" on the payroll, the company controller or an assistant may make an actual distribution of each employee paycheck. If someone has caused the preparation of a fraudulent paycheck, the guilty person will not be willing to step forward to accept the check, and evidence of the crime will be immediately apparent.

CHECK-CASHING LOSSES

Some reliable authorities state that check-cashing losses in any given year will account for about 10 percent of all crime-related losses to business. As checks and credit transactions increase, the losses suffered may also be expected to rise.

Not all these transactions involve criminal violations that are prosecuted in the courts. But if the system produces a great number of check-collection problems, a considerable amount of employee time will be wasted in running down the individuals responsible.

To avoid problems, some mail-order companies have adopted a policy of withholding shipment of merchandise until the check submitted in payment has cleared.

Business companies should be alert to the techniques used by bad-check artists, and employees should be taught to follow designated policies in cashing checks. These procedures should specify the kind of identification that must be exhibited by the customer. Obtaining a photograph and fingerprint of the passer is helpful, both as a psychological deterrent and as an investigative aid in the event the check does turn out to be fraudulent.

A check-acceptance program begins with instructions to cashiers and key employees as to how to examine the document that has been presented for cashing. The approach here may seem overly simple: Employees are told to read the check like a book, beginning at the upper left-hand corner and continuing through it, line by line and item by item. Does the name of the bank appear on the check? Is the date correct? Is the payee's name included? Is the amount written properly, both in figures and in words? Do the numerical amounts and the written amounts correspond? Is it signed? Are the issuer's name and telephone number on it, on either the back or the front? Has the issuer moved from this address? Where? Turn the check over; does the name of the payee correspond with the endorsement on the back? If the check is payable to the company, then place the company's endorsement stamp on the back. It is then the accepting employee's responsibility to list on the back of the check all numbers of identification cards presented by the issuer or passer.

A system of this kind is routine, but management must insist on blind adherence. Unless there is compliance, any retail store will accumulate a number of checks with basic errors that following the above procedure would have corrected.

Many retail stores that handle a large volume of checks now issue check-authorization cards, which are given to a customer after verification of his credit. With the aid of computer systems, a mechanical check of the card can be made in a matter of seconds

Unless cashiers and tellers are adequately briefed, they often assume that government checks and commercial money orders should be accepted without question. Although these documents are usually genuine, it should be pointed out to employees that the check or money order may be stolen or forged. The critical problem here is to make certain of the passer's identity. In cases of this kind a full year may pass before a government check is returned as a forgery by the Treasury Department. By that time the employee who accepted the check has forgotten all the details of the transaction.

COUNTERFEIT MONEY

A certain amount of counterfeit money will always be in circulation; the makers of bogus bills have been active since Colonial days. If a counterfeit bill is accepted as genuine, the business must absorb the loss. Thus it is helpful for business employees to learn to distinguish phony money from genuine. Most counterfeit bills are crudely made and can be recognized, but they may be accepted if a cashier is unconcerned or hurried.

Usually counterfeit bills are printed on an inferior grade of paper and are printed from plates of poor quality, with the flaws observable to the naked eye. To help employees distinguish counterfeit money, it is suggested that employees who handle cash take time to carefully review the free Secret Service pamphlet that shows how most bills of this type can be detected by even a cursory examination.

Criminals seldom go to the trouble to print up counterfeit bills in small denominations. It is not suggested that examination of small bills be disregarded, but loss is unlikely if a brief, but probing examination is made of bills of larger denominations.

EMPLOYEE BONDING AND THEFT INSURANCE

It has been emphasized previously that business losses from burglaries and robberies may be quite serious. But it is almost a foregone conclusion that these serious criminal losses may be dwarfed by merchandise disappearances that cannot be satisfactorily explained. Many businessmen refer to this kind of loss as "inventory shrinkage," seeming to imply that the merchandise simply disappeared into thin air. But in making an analysis of inventory problems, it is frequently difficult to trace the cause of merchandise shortages. The upshot of this is that it is often impossible to make a recovery under theft insurance policies.

Many businesses do not have theft insurance protection. In this connection it may help to use insurance as a backstop, but it should never be assumed that fidelity (theft) insurance can be used for good management controls. Although most American companies do have reasonable coverage against fire and storm losses, perhaps no more than 15 to 20 percent of these companies carry fidelity insurance protection against the wrongful acts of their own employees. Nevertheless, management may be well advised to consider both fidelity insurance and the bonding of employees, especially those who handle money or high-value items. Fidelity and bonding premiums can often be justified in a number of ways.

Many persons are unaware of the psychological deterrence that bonding of employees can provide. Insurance companies are in general agreement that employees who are aware they have been bonded are less inclined to become involved in thefts. In this situation employees somehow feel that they have more to lose. Other employees sometimes state that since they have been trusted by being placed under bond they must live up to this obligation. Also, the bonding requirement serves notice on the employee that the company has considered the possibility of theft or embezzlement in connection with his or her job.

Then, too, it may be possible to keep some individuals of questionable integrity out of the workforce by requiring employee bonding, since they may refuse to apply for a job that involves bonding as a prerequisite.

Companies that issue fidelity policies and bond their employees may help to reduce losses by making common-sense recommendations to policy holders concerning cash-handling and inventory controls. These insurance companies usually insist on good background screening by the client company's personnel department as part of the bonding application. That requirement also serves as a reminder to management that care must be exercised in the hiring process.

Businesses should not only plan to avoid bonding claims but should also be prepared to seek recovery in the event of an unforeseen loss. Individuals in management frequently express disbelief when an embezzlement or theft by trusted employees is uncovered. Sometimes this disbelief is so great that the company official cannot deal with the problem realistically even after the individual has admitted his guilt. Managers should realize that the only businesslike approach is to make whatever recovery can be obtained regardless of the position of the individual and any personal relationships that may exist.

Fidelity insurance covers only those losses caused by employee dishonesty. Since insurance companies operate on a profit-and-loss margin, they will not pay claims for losses attributable to employee theft unless it can be proved that the employee was actually involved.

When a company makes a physical count of its goods in the warehouse and finds a shortage, this in itself is not sufficient to prove employee theft to the satisfaction of the insurance company. Discrepancies of this kind frequently result from inaccurate inventory counts, poorly maintained records of stock withdrawals, bookkeeping errors, or breakage in the warehouse that is never entered in the records. Something more must be obtained to substantiate the loss. A confession, of course, will be sufficient if it can be obtained; it is preferable to have such an admission in writing.

Experience from bonding and insurance companies indicates that there is seldom a single instance of employee theft or embezzlement. If loss prevention controls are not in effect, employee dishonesty is rarely a one-time affair. It continues indefinitely until controls are applied by management.

If management discovers that an employee has committed a theft, it is important that the organization's bonding company be advised, preferably in writing. There is a standard provision in fidelity policies to the effect that the insurance company will not be obligated to pay for a dishonest or fraudulent act committed after management learns of the employee's prior dishonesty.

Therefore, a company that knowingly hires a thief or embezzler will not receive coverage on this employee even though it has paid a premium to include this individual under the fidelity bond. The fact that the thief was hired out of compassion, to give him a second chance, is of no legal consequence.

RESTITUTION

Management should be cautioned against receiving partial restitution from a thief or embezzler. When this occurs, the criminal transaction is converted into a debt situation. If the thief defaults on the balance of the restitution, the business will usually have no recourse against the insurance company unless the insurance company has agreed to accept the restitution originally offered.

PART
4

MERCHANDISE PROBLEMS

Chapter 13

Purchasing, receiving, and paying for merchandise

PURCHASING

EVERY BUSINESS STRIVES to purchase the highest-quality merchandise that management can authorize. Where possible, the purchasing function should never be controlled entirely by one individual. It is preferable for each purchase to be initiated by a written purchase order or requisition, which is subsequently matched to a written purchase order. It is recommended that each requisition be carefully screened to insure that the request is not for the personal use of an employee, and that the acquisition is actually necessary.

While seemingly obvious, this precaution is often overlooked. A Los Angeles company that never went to the trouble to check this possibility found that an employee had purchased and received merchandise worth over $100,000. Delivery was made to the employee's home address.

Other companies have frequently found that no fraud was involved but that loss has resulted from careless buying that had tied up company funds in needless overstock.

It is suggested that each purchase order contain the following information:

1. The signature of an official delegated by management with the authority to release all purchase orders.

2. The quantity of each item ordered and an accurate description

of the merchandise, including the vendor's catalog number. While this catalog number should be an integral part of the description, it should not be used in lieu of an accurate description of the merchandise.

3. The price and terms of payment agreed upon, including discounts for early payment and the amount of discount that will be allowed.

4. The time and date of purchase and the expected delivery date.

5. The name of the company employee desiring the merchandise, along with the name of the employee who accepted the order.

6. Receiving instructions, including any special conditions as to disposition of goods upon arrival.

7. A control number, issued in numerical sequence. This not only will permit internal control but will also provide an effective means of accountability after issue. The purchase order number should be shown on all packing slips, invoices, and all master cartons of merchandise where possible.

8. The complete name of the purchasing company, with address and telephone number.

9. The vendor's complete name, address, and telephone number.

It is suggested that the purchase order have sufficient copies available for the following distribution:

1. The original copy to the vendor.

2. Two copies for the individual making the purchase—one copy to be filed by purchase order number and the second copy by vendor name, category of purchase, and the like. This makes future reference much easier.

3. One copy for the accounting department, for use in verifying the vendor's invoice. This should be secured at all times to prevent alterations.

4. One copy to the receiving department to be used as a receiving document. This should be attached to the bill of lading, packing slip, or other shipping document and forwarded to the office for payment. Some companies have found it helpful to have a second copy in the receiving department for use as a receiving document if a partial shipment was received. The additional copy serves as a receiving report when the balance of the shipment comes in at a later date.

5. A follow-up copy, to be retained by the individual making the purchase. It is then filed by delivery date, or a few days prior to delivery date, so that progress of the shipment may be followed.

Additional copies of the purchase order may be deemed necessary by some companies, depending on their internal procedures. It is essential that there be a separation of management function—between the authority to purchase and the authority to pay. This, again, provides a double check on the purchasing process.

After the merchandise has been received and the transaction completed, it is suggested that the original requisition, a copy of the purchase order, and all related paperwork be maintained on file for at least one year to allow for internal auditing and verification of the control processes.

All vendors should be notified that any sale made to the company must be accompanied by a purchase order and that any sale that does not comply with this requirement will not be honored.

Serious consideration should be given to bonding all individuals who are authorized to make purchases. Although this procedure is not followed by many companies, it does provide additional protection.

All open purchase orders should be reviewed at least on a monthly basis; to provide better control, it is suggested that this be done twice each month. In some cases, it may be determined that the merchandise is no longer needed, and such a review may allow a company to cancel such an order prior to shipment.

Competitive bids should be obtained on purchases in excess of a set amount of money, such as purchases for fixed assets. A written explanation should be required to fully explain the activities of the purchasing agent when the lowest bid is not used or when there is failure to obtain bids.

A member of management, independent of those authorized to make purchases, should periodically review the prices actually paid to verify that vendors are not charging in excess of current market prices.

Particular attention should be given to those orders in which not all the merchandise is received at one time, in order to avoid the payment of duplicate invoices.

RECEIVING

Many businesses have experienced losses because they paid for merchandise that never reached the warehouse. The only way such a loss can be avoided is to make sure that the ordered quantity has been received prior to payment of the invoice.

Usually the receiving area of a large company may be an active, complex operation. There is a good possibility for loss unless receiving can be conducted as an orderly, controlled activity.

To avoid confusion, some companies limit receiving to certain specific hours of the day and insist that this schedule be followed. This not only leads to improved efficiency but allows the receiving department of the warehouse to concentrate on the receiving function. Large companies sometimes receive on a predetermined schedule, declining to accept merchandise that is not delivered at the specified time. Most smaller companies do not insist on such a rigid schedule; however, they wisely refuse to accept deliveries unless qualified employees are available for this function.

Whether the merchandise is received by railroad boxcar, company truck, or common carrier, the basic principles involved are the same. It is essential that the total order be received or accounted for and that the entire shipment be brought into the warehouse and securely stored.

One of the problems here is that there is seldom enough warehouse help to bring merchandise inside immediately. Therefore, employees should be taught to bring in items of small size and of high value at the first opportunity. Dock workers should understand that all merchandise may be tempting to a thief but that some items are so bulky or heavy that merchandise should be brought inside on a selective basis; in other words, smaller, valuable items, which are easier for a thief to grab and run off with, should be given top priority.

Counting the order

Experience shows that losses can be expected unless the shipment is accurately counted at the first opportunity. There are two distinct counting processes involved here. The first of these is the package count. This is the number of boxes, barrels, bales, and so forth that is received when the deliveryman places the merchandise on the dock. If the proper number of pieces is not received, an exception report should be made immediately. A second counting procedure is used when the merchandise is brought inside and the boxes are broken open. The receiving clerk then counts the number of pieces or items of each kind in the shipment.

In making these counts, the receiving clerk should not work in more than 25-block counts, as experience shows it is easy to confuse the total when dealing with larger multiples. Every effort should also be made to finish counts without outside distractions. If a truck driver making a delivery succeeds in interrupting the count, there is greater likelihood for confusion. Most drivers are, of course, honest, conscientious people. There are always a few, however, who would not hesitate to withhold merchandise if there is an opportunity to confuse the receiving clerk.

As a control procedure, some companies ask the deliveryman to make a count of his own. After the receiving clerk has completed his examination, he then asks the driver to furnish the driver's total, without revealing his own count. If the two figures are not identical, the practice here is for the driver and the receiving clerk to both recheck the load together, until they are in agreement that an accurate figure has been reached.

One of the basics here is to make certain that the receiving clerk understands that his company is legally obliged to pay for the merchandise that he signs for on a shipping document and that errors can be costly.

If the incoming freight is of a kind that has been ordered by weight, rather than by unit, then the receiving count should also be based on weight.

One type of fraud that has persisted over the years involves placing additional weights on the vehicle carrying the merchandise and somehow removing those weights between the time that the loaded vehicle is driven on the scales and the time that the empty vehicle is weighed.

Receiving in a properly controlled area

Ideally, merchandise should be received on an inner dock, protected against the weather. Losses attributable to rain or wind are frequently observed in unprotected receiving areas, even in mild climates.

It is usually preferable to receive through a rear or side area of the building rather than through the front door. In many large city locations this cannot be avoided. The logic here is that it may be difficult to supervise the deliveryman at all times and that he may have unsupervised access to goods in retail sales areas. There is always an increased possibility that the deliveryman may injure a customer or interfere with customer access through the front door of the building.

The short count

If a truck driver is dishonest, he may deliberately fail to unload all the cartons on his truck. There are times when some boxes in the shipment may be used to support the end of an unloading conveyor inside the truck, and these articles may be conveniently "forgotten" in the delivery truck. A short count will be revealed, of course, if the receiving clerk counts accurately. One of the best preventive measures available is to provide adequate lighting for the interior of the delivery truck or trailer and to insist that receiving employees use adequate lighting. Portable floodlights or beams should be utilized as standard receiving equipment.

USE A SEPARATE SHIPPING DOCK

Many retail stores have little need for a separate shipping dock unless there are interstore transfers between other facilities in the same business. Confusion frequently results if the company must use one dock for both outgoing and incoming shipments.

If only one dock is available, it may be separated into two areas by a portable fence mounted on wheels in such a way that the fence can be shifted up and down the dock floor. Some companies have installed rolldown-type steel doors that are fastened to the dock floor. When not used to separate the dock, these doors are left in the overhead position.

There is some difference of opinion, but most professional warehouse superintendents feel that it is better to have one central receiving area than to separate receiving facilities in the various departments of one business.

Original purchase order as the receiving report

Some companies receive without any documentation whatever, counting the merchandise and comparing it with the notations on the packing slip inside the shipment. Experience shows that in many instances the packing slip is difficult to read. Often, the packing slip figure does not correspond with either the quantity or the quality of the merchandise in the shipment. If the packing slip count is accepted as accurate, then the receiver is, in effect, condoning whatever errors may have been made by the shipper.

Receiving blind

As a loss prevention control, it is preferable for the receiving clerk to "receive blind." This means that the receiving clerk should count the contents of each box before referring to the packer's invoice or packing list. After the count has been made, a comparison is in order with the packer's list. If the two do not correspond, a recount should be made.

Many companies use a copy of the original purchase order as a receiving report. If the quantities listed on this particular copy have been blanked out, then the receiving clerk will be required to count quantities. A system of this kind will usually insure an independent count, although the packing slip may be accepted by the receiving clerk if the purchase order used as a receiving report shows the quantity ordered.

If the company receives from the packing slip only, it will sometimes be found that suppliers take advantage of the company by shipping merchandise that was never ordered. Since warehouse space is at a premium and merchandise must be turned over in order to make money, many companies find that receiving must be coordinated with purchasing.

One disadvantage in having receiving clerks be unaware of the quantity ordered is that a discrepancy between the quantities ordered and the quantities received might not otherwise be apparent until the accounting office compares the purchase order with the receiving report. By the time this takes place, the incoming merchandise has almost always been placed into stock, thus making a recheck impossible.

Handling the receiving report

If two copies of the purchase order are provided to the receiving department, one can be returned to accounting for comparison with the purchase order and the supplier's invoice. A good control system requires that the receiving report be forwarded directly to the accounts payable clerk rather than to the purchasing department. If the report should go back to the purchasing department, there is a possibility that the receiving record could be altered prior to being sent on for payment. Experience shows that this is an area where there could be fraudulent collusion between the purchasing agent and the supplier. If a second copy of the purchase order is provided to the receiving department, one can be retained as a receiving report on a partial shipment, while the second copy remains in the receiving file until the balance of the shipment is received.

Management verification

It is suggested the management make regular, unscheduled audits of merchandise received in the warehouse. The inspection should include an actual count of the goods received after the receiving clerk has signed for the merchandise, but before the items have actually been placed into stock. Verification serves to emphasize the need for employees to make accurate counts in every instance.

Where delivery is to be made

If there is any question, the purchase order should include definite instructions as to where the shipment is to be made. Every year insurance bonding companies report cases in which deliveries are made to the home address of an employee. In most instances of this kind, the merchandise is paid for by the company but never actually finds its way into the company warehouse.

Incomplete shipments

If the quantity of merchandise received is incomplete, the specific amount received should be marked on the receiving report. If a copy of the purchase order is used as a receiving report, the purchase order should be refiled in the receiving clerk's suspense file of unreceived shipments. A second copy of the purchase order will serve to advise accounts payable of the quantities received. The copy of the purchase order that remains in the receiving clerk's file can be used to reflect receipt of the balance of the order.

Some companies recommend that a receiving supervisor be notified as soon as a count has been made or a shipment completely unloaded. In a situation of this kind the supervisor usually checks the truck or railroad car to satisfy himself that no merchandise has been left inside the trailer or boxcar.

Frequently, a supplier is unable to furnish the exact merchandise ordered. Unless the receiving department is alert, a substitution may not be detected, and the supplier may be paid for a more expensive item than the merchandise actually received.

Overshipments

Some companies refuse to accept excess merchandise, since they will be required to pay for items that they may be unable to sell in the immediate future. This policy may vary from business to business. In any event, the delivery driver will ask the receiving clerk to indicate that a specific number of pieces were delivered in excess of the amounts listed on the freight bill.

When an overshipment is discovered, it is always possible that the receiving clerk will place the merchandise into stock, hoping that he will not be required to account for the excess. When an opportunity is available, the receiving clerk will then load the extra merchandise in his personal car or ship it to his home through collusion with a truck driver.

Another possibility is that a dishonest employee in the receiving department may manipulate merchandise that is found to be short at the time of arrival. In one instance the missing box was valued at approximately $20. Other boxes in the same shipment were valued in excess of $2,000 each. When it was discovered that the shipment was short one piece, the receiving employee then replaced the article valued at $20, simultaneously removing one of the packages valued at approximately $2,000. This substitution was discovered eventually, since the truck driver making the delivery had made a specific note as to which article was missing on the shipper's copy of the bill of lading.

Placing merchandise into stock

In some companies it will be observed that sales employees go direct to the receiving dock to remove merchandise because a customer is impatient. It is recommended that this procedure not be allowed, unless it is absolutely essential. Merchandise should be actually added to the existing stock in the warehouse or receiving counts will be confused by allowing sales employees to remove items from the dock.

Damage claims

The receiving clerk should make certain that the delivery driver signs the purchasing company's copy of the freight bill reflecting damaged merchandise. Receiving employees should be trained to watch out for warped or punctured packages, water-stained cartons, or broken packages. Another indication of damage is a container that has had items spilled against it while sitting in the delivery truck. Unless an orderly, regular procedure is used for filing claims, it may be discovered that damaged merchandise will be placed in the warehouse, and there may be no recourse against the supplier.

Intracompany transfers of merchandise

Some companies use careful controls in receiving from outside suppliers but are lax in receiving merchandise from warehouses or stores within their own organization. "After all," the rationalization goes, "I know that our company uses careful shipping procedures, so I can rely on their counts."

If it should become known to the shipper that no count is being made, there is a temptation to ship short and steal the merchandise that was not included.

Another problem may arise when a district manager or other company official loads merchandise into his personal car for delivery to a store that has an immediate need for a particular item. Unless proper documents are prepared to show that the merchandise was transferred from one store and received at another, the inventory of each store will be out of balance.

Then, too, if a district official is allowed to shift merchandise from one location to another, there is always the possibility that he may conceal a number of boxes in his garage or somewhere along the route, delivering only a fraction of the items picked up. The district official is taking little risk if he knows that accountability is not properly maintained.

Company procedures should also require regular processing of packages addressed to a company official. If members of management object to having their packages opened, they should have personal items sent to their home address. In like manner, controls should be used on packages carried out of the office by any employee. Unless this precaution is followed, supervisors or management personnel may wrap warehouse merchandise, take it to the office, and carry it out the front door.

Improvements in controls and procedures

There is good reason for believing that the receiving process should be handled by experienced, proven employees who understand the system. Regular employees usually have more to lose by failing to count incoming shipments or by disregarding receiving practices.

There are some expenditures for intangibles that should be examined whenever management seeks to determine whether value has actually been received for all invoices submitted by suppliers. It is usually a comparatively simple matter to audit the receipt of merchandise, since physical items can be counted, checked, and placed into stock or into a store room.

Radio and TV advertising is an example of this kind of intangible. A script that was actually used can normally be retained in file, along with some supporting information. Newspaper advertising may be authorized and paid for, but frequently there is nothing in file that a company auditor can use for verification a short time after the ad was run. This is not to imply that there is reason to doubt the honesty of advertising employees. But it may be better to retain news-paper tearsheets, proofs, or actual clippings in a documentation file.

PAYING FOR GOODS RECEIVED

As a general rule, merchandise should never be paid for in advance, unless needed goods cannot be obtained in any other way. One reason is that the buyer may not do his best to meet the customer's specifications once the money is in hand. In addition, the purchaser may not be able to obtain repayment from the seller if the merchandise does not meet specifications.

A Los Angeles company recently had an urgent need for a type of East Indian spice that was hard to locate on the open market. To make certain that a supply was on hand, the company paid $12,000 for the spice prior to delivery. A few days after the buyer's check was cashed, it was discovered that the supplier was a dummy company set up to make fraudulent sales. By the time this was discovered, the individuals connected with the dummy firm had disappeared.

Verification of delivery

Some businesses make a practice of writing checks to the supplier prior to the time that proof of delivery has been received in the purchaser's office. There are a number of reasons why this is done. The accounts payable clerk may be merely trying to clear his desk. Frequently, a bill may be paid within a specific time limit to take advantage of a 2 percent discount or to curry favor with the supplier. A good basic policy, however, is to withhold payment until proof has been received that goods were actually received, as billed. In the event some of the material in the shipment was received in a damaged condition, or the shipment is short, it is suggested that payment be withheld for that part of the order that was not satisfactory.

Another good policy is to make payment on original suppliers' invoices only. If checks are written on the basis of duplicate invoices or vendors' statements, it is possible that the supplier's original invoice has already been processed and that a second (double) payment may be made.

Conditions that should be met before payment

There are three conditions that should be satisfied before a supplier's invoice is paid. First, there should be satisfactory evidence of purchase. The supplier's invoice should be compared with the accounts payable open-purchase-order file, to which the receiving report should be affixed. The invoice, purchase order, and receiving report should be in agreement as to specifications of the item shipped, the quantity received, and the price charged. In the event these three documents are not in agreement, the invoice should be forwarded to the purchasing department with information pertaining to the discrepancy. If the discrepancy is nominal, it may not be necessary to issue a supplement to the purchase order. In that case, the purchasing manager may have authority to make corrections, if company policy permits. It is suggested that a supplement be issued to the purchase order if any substantial amount of money is involved.

Purchase orders are not always issued for the goods or services represented by some invoices. In a situation of this kind, it is suggested that the invoice be forwarded to the company official authorized to approve this expenditure. As the approval of this official usually serves both as a purchase order and a receiving report, due caution should be used to make certain that the goods or services represented by the invoice were actually delivered.

Verification of the receipt of merchandise is the second requirement that should be satisfied before an invoice is paid. If the company has a consistent policy for preparing receiving reports on all items coming into the business, then the receiving report will usually represent documentary proof that the merchandise arrived in good condition.

There should be no exception to the rule that merchandise is to be received by the receiving department. Specifications, quantities, and method of shipment should be verified by comparison with the purchase order. The receiving report, completely filled out and signed, should be sent to the accounts payable department, where it is held with the purchase order until an invoice arrives from the supplier. If the company does not use a receiving report, the receiving clerk should acknowledge receipt of the merchandise by an appropriate notation on the bill of lading, delivery ticket, or transportation bill.

The third requirement is validation of the invoice. The accounts payable clerk should make sure that the terms set out on the purchase order are those that appear on the invoice. Additions and extensions should then be verified to make certain that the invoice is not being overpaid. If the supplier offers a cash discount, it is suggested that this be verified and a notation placed on the invoice, along with the net amount payable.

If the terms of the invoice do not correspond with those of the purchase order, the buyer should be governed by those on the purchase order, unless the terms on the supplier's invoice appear to be to the buyer's advantage.

When the buyer has agreed to pay freight on the purchase, the freight bill should be verified with the receiving report and should also be compared with the purchase order before payment.

When all three requirements for payment of the supplier's invoice have been completed, all the documentary verification should be stapled together and a form placed on the front of the assembled paperwork. It is suggested that a printed form like the one shown in Figure 5 be used. This work form should be filled out by the employee in the accounts payable section. When the work has been verified, the employee should place his or her initials on the appropriate part of the form, indicating that the invoice has been authenticated for payment.

Cancellation of supporting documents and invoices

There is always a possibility that a supplier may be paid twice for one invoice. Proper controls therefore require that the invoice and supporting documents be canceled in some manner so that a resubmission would be immediately apparent. Perhaps the safest way to handle the cancellation is to use a mechanical perforator that punches holes through the invoice and all supporting documents and imprints "paid" through all the papers.

Figure 5. Invoice verification form.

INVOICE VERIFICATION
Purchase Order No. _____
Receiving Report _____
Price _____
Extensions _____
_____ Processed by

Some companies use a rubber stamp to mark invoices "paid"; however, if the stamp is placed along the edge of the invoice receiving report or other supporting documents, someone could cut off the stamped impression and resubmit the documents for a fraudulent second payment.

Credit memos

It is suggested that credit memos obtained from suppliers be processed through the accounting department immediately and that the credit deducted from the next payment be made to that supplier. Some suppliers are not used with great regularity, however, and a letter should be written to the supplier in such a case, requesting that he or she forward a check by return mail to cancel the credit memo.

Chapter
14

Warehousing

IN THE RETAIL or wholesale operation, perhaps the bulk of a company's assets may consist of goods in stores, warehouses, or stockrooms. It is quite obvious, of course, that there must be adequate controls to regulate receiving, storage, and shipping of merchandise, especially in warehouse and stockroom areas.

In a warehouse operation, business losses may occur in direct relation to the conditions under which employees are asked to work. Lack of order, poor organization and warehousing methods, inadequate lighting, trash accumulation, and lack of sanitary facilities may all contribute to a lack of respect for the true worth of company goods. Such conditions may lead employees to the false impression that merchandise is of little value.

No one knows for certain, but some authorities believe that up to 85 percent of stolen cargo is carried away from freight transfer locations and warehouses by individuals who have authorization to be on that part of the premises. If management is able to exercise reasonable regulation, many of these problems will be eliminated.

Overcrowded conditions on the dock frequently lead to increased theft problems and warehouse record errors. If the physical areas are inadequate, management should consider rearranging or enlarging dock areas, as well as inside storage locations.

Only cargo-handling vehicles or trucks should be allowed inside the company receiving area. This means that visitor and employee parking lot areas should be located on another part of the property.

If a fence has not been provided for the dock area, employee vehicles should be restricted to areas that are definitely away from the warehouse doors or receiving dock areas.

Then, too, it is recommended that access through warehouse doors be restricted, consistent with the needs of the business. If visiting deliverymen are not restricted, there is a possibility that they may carry away merchandise. Usually, deliverymen can be effectively controlled when they have access to restroom facilities, a water fountain, and vending machines that can be reached without going through the warehouse.

Many companies can document specific instances of thefts that occurred because warehouse doors were left open and unsupervised during break periods or lunch. If it is considered necessary that doors be left open for ventilation, then a woven-wire mesh door, locked into place, will restrict access while providing good circulation.

Some dock thieves are so brazen as to grab articles while employees are working on the dock. Perhaps most thefts on a dock take place while employees are handling assignments in other parts of the warehouse. Situations of this kind can often be prevented by stationing a uniformed guard on the outside dock until all merchandise shipments are brought inside the warehouse.

Some other problems are observed time and again in warehouse after warehouse. The report of a loss prevention consultant at a Phoenix, Arizona, warehouse is typical:

> There were two ten-foot-by-twenty-foot framed screens that were locked in the freight-loading doors to provide ventilation. It was noted that one of the screens had a hole cut through the wire, approximately 14 by 16 inches in size. There appeared to be no purpose for the hole, except to pass out company merchandise.

THE PERPETUAL INVENTORY SYSTEM

In controlling merchandise, one of the most effective tools from a loss prevention standpoint has been the perpetual inventory system. The following are some of the advantages:

1. Management can usually detect inventory shortages or overages almost immediately after they occur. This enables an investigation to be made promptly, considerably increasing the likelihood of arriving at the cause of the variance.

2. Sales, purchasing, and warehouse officials know what is in the warehouse and what can be delivered to a customer. Purchasing con-

centrates on items that are needed, and customer satisfaction is improved.

3. Management is able to detect variances between outgoing shipments and sales receipts, and between purchases and goods actually received.

4. Employees are aware that shortages will be quickly brought to the attention of management.

REGULAR INVENTORIES

A regular inventory check of warehouse or stockroom merchandise is an advisable loss control procedure. A San Francisco cigarette and candy warehouse experienced frequent, unexplained shortages until a system of this kind was adopted. When the system was instigated, it took more than five weeks to get merchandise totals straightened out. Thereafter, there were no serious discrepancies for more than four years, although counts were made on a two-week basis.

Management of this company stated that over the years employees had gotten into the habit of "taking a few smokes," as one of the job benefits. With the new inventory system, employees realized that shortages would be immediately investigated. Losses shrank to four or five cartons of cigarettes a month. It was apparent that employees had gone from "taking a few smokes" to carrying out large quantities of merchandise, and that the problem had been corrected.

"BROKEN" PACKAGES

Some warehouses have experienced loss in merchandise inventories only after they began selling broken lots of candy, cigarettes, and similar items. The same situation may exist with a wholesale electrical company that warehouses broken cartons of electric shavers. Broken cartons should be kept in a high-value cage. By returning to a policy of selling only unbroken, original units, some companies have corrected this problem.

SALES DEALS AND PROMOTIONS

In addition to their usual sales responsibilities, some salesmen are allowed to offer deals or promotions. These usually involve special price reductions on large-lot sales or valuable merchandise prizes to the purchasing agent of the buyer. Inventory paperwork controls may be disrupted if the salesman is not careful in distinguishing between deals and regular sales. Unexplained sales at special markdowns may cause inventory totals to reflect shortages when there is only a paperwork snarl.

If merchandise items are given away as part of a promotion, it is up to the individual salesman to submit records that explain away the apparent shortage.

As a general proposition, some management officials state that approval for deals or promotions should be limited to as few salesmen as possible. In many instances, promotions are authorized by high-ranking officials within a business organization, after careful consideration and study of market conditions. Some companies have found it helpful to devise a special document that will allow adjustment of inventory records and values after management approval.

CONTROL OF WAREHOUSE INVOICES

Regardless of the company's delivery system or method of preparation, a shipping invoice is the document that authorizes the legitimate delivery of merchandise. In effect, it is a blank check against company assets, and should be treated with due regard. The shipping invoice (warehouse invoice) may serve as a selection form, customer copy, control form, billing copy, and/or driver's copy for delivery. Because of these multiple uses, it is recommended that the invoice be preprinted, numerically controlled, and used in numerical blocks for each day's delivery. A comparison should be made of all returned copies signed by the customer with the office billing or control copy. This should reveal whether any of the numerically controlled invoices is unaccounted for. If an invoice is missing, an investigation should be undertaken immediately.

Depending on the system followed, invoices should be prepared with three or four copies:

1. The customer's copy, which must be left with the customer, indicating delivery of merchandise.
2. The driver's copy, which will be used by the driver for accuracy of delivery, signed by the customer, and returned for comparison with the control or billing copy at the end of the day's deliveries.

3. The office billing copy, which may also act as a control copy.
4. The office control copy, which should be reviewed and compared with the driver's signed, returned copy to verify that all deliveries have been billed or monies collected.

SELECTION AND CHECKING

Ideally, selection of merchandise should be made from a copy of the invoice. The selector, or "picker," should select merchandise from the warehouse and enter quantities on the invoice. Some warehouses maintain controls by circling a section of the invoice in red, with a minus figure to indicate that the proper quantity of merchandise is unavailable in the warehouse. When this is done, the driver will know that his load will be short. It will be apparent to him what the shortage consists of, and he will be able to explain this shortage to the customer. To maintain responsibility, it is desirable for the selector to initial the invoice, acknowledging that he filled the order or made a notation to the effect that proper quantities were not available.

For effective controls, an independent count of the merchandise selected should be made by a checker; this checker should be an employee other than the selector. Whenever practical, actual checking should be done at the time the merchandise is being loaded onto the delivery vehicle. Errors observed by the checker should be immediately brought to the attention of supervision. If the value involved is considerable, the vehicle can be unloaded at that time and a verification made for accuracy. Insofar as practical, the driver should also be present at the time of loading so that he cannot subsequently claim that he was loaded short. The driver should verify the checker's work and sign the invoice, acknowledging responsibility for the load. The checker, too, should also initial the invoice, accepting responsibility for this part of the operation.

There are three common types of errors in shipping from warehouses: shortages, overages, and improper selection of merchandise.

A recommended control system involves the maintenance of a file, by invoice number, indicating whether the selector made an error, whether both the selector and the checker made an error that was caught by the driver, and whether the driver returned overages or an improper selection of merchandise. If a file of this kind is carefully maintained, it may be possible to pinpoint a trend reflecting dishonesty, conspiracy, or carelessness on the part of selectors, checkers, and drivers.

A card index may be maintained by employees, fixing responsibility for errors to a particular selector, checker, or driver. A frequency rate system of this kind will inform management as to the frequency with which a particular employee makes errors, the type of error, the kind of merchandise involved, and the value.

Frequently, errors made by selectors and checkers can be seriously reduced if information from the frequency rate system is used by supervision as a management tool. Often, employees do not fully understand that loss may result from overshipment, undershipment, or selection of the wrong type of merchandise. Then too, it may be discovered that some employees are error-prone; they should be given other assignments. It is easy to "give away merchandise" unless management can reduce shipping errors.

MERCHANDISE STACKING

A loss prevention consultant sometimes observes that merchandise is broken or damaged in the warehouse because of poor stacking practices.

Unless warehouse employees are appropriately trained, it will be observed that they frequently stack boxes to great heights with a forklift. When this happens, it is usually a matter of time until some of the boxes collapse into the warehouse aisles. This practice can lead to serious losses. Merchandise may not be damaged when it falls but a warehouse employee may be killed or seriously injured. The lawsuit that could be anticipated from such a tragic incident could result in considerable costs.

THE SECURITY ROOM

Shipments are, of course, far less likely to be stolen after they are brought inside the protective walls of the company warehouse. Extra protection may be justified, however, if the merchandise is of unusual value, if it is small and easily concealed, and if it has a ready sale on the black market.

Many companies use a security room or high-value cage for such merchandise, locating this locked holding room within an inner area of the warehouse. It may be advisable to have the door under the visual control of the warehouse superintendent's office. Ideally, access should be restricted to two or three dependable employees, with key control rigidly supervised.

WAREHOUSE PALLETS

While retaining good control over merchandise, a company may sustain a loss of the wooden pallets on which merchandise is warehoused or shipped. It is, of course, easier to load shipments by placing a pallet of freight into the delivery truck. If this practice is followed, some system should be used for the accountability of pallets.

It may be advisable to mark the company name on each pallet, by stencil and spray paint.

Unable to rationalize the continued loss of pallets, a Minneapolis company discovered that one supervisor was making no effort to repair broken pallets. Instead, the employee was breaking up damaged pallets and carrying home the pieces of hardwood for his fireplace.

A major meat packing company found that pallets were consistently lost until it began billing for pallets along with the company's meat products. When the pallets are returned, appropriate credit is given.

MERCHANDISE RETURNED FOR CREDIT

Unless good controls are used, it may be relatively easy for a company deliveryman to issue false credits to an outside business. It is essential that there be verification that merchandise was actually returned before credit is allowed.

A suggested system here makes use of a four-part color, numerically controlled form to record credits. The recommended system is as follows:

1. If merchandise is refused or given back to the driver for return, the driver should write up the credit, clearly indicating the reason. The driver should then request the customer to sign the unseparated credit document and give the customer the first carbon copy. From practical experience, some businesses report that the customer should not be given the original to prevent forgery.

2. When the deliveryman returns to the warehouse, he should provide the remaining unseparated copies to the supervisor at the time he checks in his money and merchandise.

3. The supervisor should verify the accuracy of the credit by physically counting the items being returned. The supervisor should then remove the original and one copy of the credit form, attaching the deliveryman's control copy to the merchandise itself.

4. The original of the credit document should be sent to the

office, and the last copy should remain with the merchandise itself for return to stock at a later time.

5. An assigned employee from the stockroom should verify the accuracy of the return by comparing the merchandise with the credit document; he should show his approval by signing the credit document form. This signed copy should then be routed to the office for comparison with the original. If there is office verification, it will be apparent that the merchandise was checked in by a supervisor, was re-verified by the assigned stockroom employee, has been found in salable condition, and has been returned to the warehouse shelves.

6. One copy of the credit form may be filed in the customer's folder and one maintained in the office in a file for each deliveryman. By this method, a frequency rate can be maintained to show whether the driver has a disproportionate number of credits. If so, an immediate investigation should be undertaken by management. In addition, it is essential that the credit form also be routed through inventory records so that the returned merchandise can be added to the warehouse inventory.

Companies that do not maintain good control over merchandise returned for credit have found that some employees regard this kind of merchandise as belonging to no one. As a consequence, employees may be tempted to steal the merchandise.

In Vernon, California, a cigar and cigarette wholesaler stored returned goods on open shelves between the receiving department and the warehouse wall outside the manager's office. The articles on the shelves were cartons of cigarette lighters, boxes of cigars, candy, and specialty items that had not been placed back into stock. Over the years employees began to help themselves to this merchandise, and management never objected. Employees who would never have considered theft from the warehouse seemed to see nothing wrong in taking returned goods. When the ownership of this company changed, the new manager had a considerable problem convincing employees that this merchandise should be protected as carefully as all other assets.

SALESMEN'S SAMPLES

Many companies have found that sales may be increased if salesmen are able to furnish samples to selected buyers. On the other hand, some companies have been surprised to add up the cost of samples that were given away indiscriminately by salesmen.

To what extent samples should be used is obviously a management problem.

It is recommended that salesmen not be allowed to pick up samples in the warehouse without appropriate controls. An electronics company in the San Francisco area noted that the warehouse was always found unlocked after company sales meetings. One of the officials in charge of sales always unlocked the warehouse and allowed salesmen to load up shopping carts with any items that appeared to be useful samples. It was eventually found that warehouse inventory figures showed a sizable shortage because of this practice.

At another electronics wholesale company salesmen did not actually pick up samples themselves. They merely typed out shipping labels for "customers" and gave warehouse employees the list of items that were to be shipped to those "customers" as sales samples. Warehouse employees who made these shipments were never aware that the addresses on the shipping labels were not customers. Because of such practices, it is suggested that no shipments be made from the warehouse except those controlled by regular sales order or shipping invoice forms, of the kind used for all company shipments. If items are listed on these sales order forms or shipping documents, spot checks by management would reveal whether the transactions were legitimate.

COMPANY FOOD OR MEDICAL PRODUCTS

Not all inventory losses involve the removal of stock from the premises. Some businesses are vulnerable to unauthorized employee consumption or use on the job. In a typical situation, employees of a wholesale drug company may open cartons containing cold remedies, aspirin, or vitamins.

If this type of consumption is regarded as an employee benefit, the company will absorb the cost. Too often, however, management has no definite controls over merchandise and does not pay sufficient attention to realize what is taking place.

It is suggested that management formulate policies and adhere to them closely. A candy company in Utah allowed employees to consume candy if packages were accidentally broken open. When losses seemed unreasonable, management found that the forklift operator in the warehouse was deliberately ripping open cartons to create broken packages for the other employees. Losses were reduced sharply when management adopted a policy that required destruction of all broken packages.

LUNCH WAGON EMPLOYEES

In some industrial, retail, or wholesale installations, a lunch wagon or lunch service representative is allowed to come and go in the company building. In some cases the lunch service employee has helped himself to company merchandise. Access controls may therefore be recommended. In a few industrial companies it has been observed that employees trade small merchandise items from the warehouse for sandwiches and other edibles on the lunch wagon. The cumulative effect of this activity could be serious.

SALVAGE

Some companies do not insist that damaged merchandise be returned for inspection. To prevent freight charges for shipping the merchandise back to the supplier, these companies generally allow a salesman or other representatives to look at the allegedly defective items and grant a credit on the spot. This means that a new sale may be lost since the merchandise was still usable, even though it was so defective that it could not be sold.

As a matter of policy, however, some companies insist on controlling the salvage of their products, even though return freight charges must be paid. The same procedure may also be followed for overage merchandise. Revlon Cosmetics, for example, has merchandise returned to the company, where it is crushed and trucked away under security supervision. It is then crushed again by a bulldozer and buried underground. All this, of course, costs money, but it does result in product integrity. The attitude here is that a good product demands product protection.

If damaged or returned goods are stored in such a way that they seem to be junk, employees may assume that such items are of little value. Experience reflects that many employees were first tempted to carry away damaged merchandise. From this kind of involvement, employees may go, by steps, from taking damaged merchandise to deliberately damaging merchandise so that it may be taken, to out-and-out theft. Therefore, management needs to establish adequate warehousing methods so that damaged or returned goods do not tempt employees.

CONTROL OF THE WILL-CALL SECTION

Unless basic protective measures are established and implemented, serious losses may occur in the will-call section of any business.

Ideally, the will-call area should be a clearly designated section, segregated from warehouse and storeroom locations. If the site selected is proper, it will usually not be necessary for customers to pass by either the receiving or shipping dock. Experience indicates that this will reduce the likelihood of theft from the dock.

In addition, there should be adequate space for will-call parking, controlled by legible signs.

Collusion with customers

Unless procedures require will-call orders to be selected in advance, a will-call clerk may place extra merchandise in the order that has been set aside for a customer who is in collusion with him or her. To prevent collusion, some companies assign employees to the will-call counter for a period of three to six months, on a rotating basis. If a dishonest customer is not certain which employee will wait on him, there is less likelihood for loss.

When will-call orders must be selected prior to the customer's arrival, it is recommended that management make unannounced audits of these orders. Even where no dishonesty is involved, it may be found that the employee is error-prone. If it is found that a greater quantity or more expensive merchandise has been included, it is suggested that the selector be counseled by management or supervision. This should be done only if it appears that this was an honest error. Bad selection may cost the company money or may be destructive of customer relationships, which is perhaps an even more costly loss.

To be effective, management audits of the merchandise selected should be held at irregular, unannounced times. If fraud appears to be a distinct possibility, then a close scrutiny of counter sales may be in order.

Fraudulently placed orders

Both local and national companies have experienced loss when swindlers have impersonated regular customers in picking up merchandise. These situations usually involve orders received by telephone for pickup at the will-call counter. In most cases, inside sales representatives are acquainted with the persons who call in orders. At least, inside sales employees usually recognize a current purchase order number that may be furnished by the caller. But when orders are received from a great number of persons, the possibility for fraud may increase.

If the messenger picking up the will-call merchandise is not known to the clerk on duty, some companies require the will-call clerk to ask the name of the person who placed the order. Where this procedure is followed, the name of the individual making the order has already been written on the sales ticket, which is not observable by the person requesting the order. If the individual claiming the merchandise is unable to furnish the name of the person who ordered the shipment, then the will-call clerk does not make delivery until telephone verification can be made with the caller.

A good system is to require the person claiming the merchandise to furnish a driver's license or other reliable document that will establish identity.

Because of loss experience, some companies have adopted a commercial device that incorporates a photograph of the will-call ticket, along with a picture of the individual making the pickup, and his or her driver's license. Photographs are not developed unless there is a loss.

Return of merchandise to stock

Procedures should be in effect to verify that merchandise is returned to stock if a will-call order is not picked up within a reasonable time. A Philadelphia company neglected this procedure and eventually discovered that will-call clerks were taking home merchandise from canceled orders.

The cash register

A cash register should be used at the will-call counter to assist in maintaining accountability. If more than one clerk is assigned to the will-call section, it is preferable for each clerk to be assigned an individual drawer or cash box.

In one store a thief boldly grabbed a cash register from the will-call counter, threw it into the back of a pickup truck, and made off before the startled clerk realized what was happening. To avoid incidents of this kind, it is suggested that the cash register be bolted to the counter or secured so that it cannot be readily carried away.

Shipping

EXTENSIVE EXPERIENCE shows that merchandise should never be shipped without adequate documentation. Boxes or packages awaiting transportation should be adequately protected and should never remain on an outside dock without supervision. In the typical theft pattern, "outside" drivers simply place unsupervised merchandise into their own load. But company drivers may also be guilty. Many companies have found that the only adequate procedure is to require a warehouse supervisor to check off each box or package placed on the truck, with a second employee (other than the driver) doing the actual loading.

CONTROLLING SHIPPING AREAS

Supervisors and warehouse managers should make certain that only authorized delivery and shipping vehicles are allowed in the shipping areas. Visitor and employee parking lots should be located in an area that is physically separated from the docks, and relatives should not be allowed to wait in a loading area to pick up employees who are about to go off shift.

Many companies claim that it is impractical or even impossible to limit access to the interior of the warehouse. But companies that have tried this procedure report that it can be done. Inventory shrinkage figures usually prove convincingly that management can insist that access be granted on a "need" basis only.

Truck drivers do need unrestricted access to a telephone to call their company dispatcher, as well as access to restroom facilities and a water fountain and vending machines. In planning warehouse accommodations, it is suggested that these facilities be located immediately adjacent to the dock where drivers and shippers park their vehicles.

Restrictive signs should be posted and drivers should be told that they are strictly limited to certain areas. A driver who refuses to abide by these instructions should not be allowed to handle freight at that location, and his company supervisor or dispatcher should be so informed.

PRELOADING DELIVERY TRUCKS

Many businesses must load delivery trucks on the day prior to departure. Delivery is often a time-consuming process, and customers cannot wait for loading to take place after regular work crews report for duty. If loading takes place during night hours, the overtime pay involved may be considerable, and supervision may be difficult to maintain. This, of course, may be the only answer with perishable merchandise that is not kept under refrigeration.

Many companies meet this problem by preloading trucks on the afternoon shift, as soon as the driver returns from a run. Loaded with merchandise, the truck is then left overnight in a fenced yard. Some companies have followed a procedure of this kind for years without experiencing problems, but others have not been so fortunate. Regardless of a favorable loss experience in this situation, it may be desirable for management to reassess the problem.

A Los Angeles industrial linen supply company preloaded linen delivery trucks for years, leaving them overnight in a well-fenced yard. An ex-convict who lived with one of the women production workers in the plant had a fancied grievance against management. This difficulty originated because the plant superintendent had ignored the ex-convict's demand that the woman's paycheck be turned over to him.

Climbing over the fence in the middle of the night, the ex-convict found the keys in the ignition of the preloaded vehicle. The yard was located on a well-lighted street, and the fence was well constructed. Ignoring the passing cars, the ex-convict proceeded to methodically batter the fence until he flattened two of the heavy pipe posts that supported the wire-mesh fence. Driving the vehicle over the fence, the ex-convict scattered linen worth about $16,000 by throwing it into sewer openings and storm drains over a wide area. An additional outlay of money was eventually needed to repair the battered truck and rebuild the fence.

A methodical procedure for locking each vehicle inside the fenced yard may provide additional security. This is often found to be inadequate if there is no alarm on the fence or the individual trucks or if there is no guard service.

Some companies have adopted some other alternatives. One company in the Santa Ana, California, area allows the company driver to take the preloaded company vehicle to his own residence. The driver then parks the company truck on the street directly in front of his residence, making certain that it is locked. If the driver is an employee of proven reliability, the plan may have some merit. Experience shows, however, that neighbors are usually aware when the driver and his family are absent for the night, and one of them might take advantage of the situation to loot the truck.

A San Francisco meat packing plant has a guard post at its main building. Meat trucks are preloaded and locked inside a fenced yard about two blocks away. Drivers may be required to leave at odd hours of the night, and keys for the fenced yard and the vehicles are maintained on a board inside the guard station. When the driver begins his run, he obtains keys by presenting his company identification card to the guard on duty. The weakness here is that there is always turnover among the guard personnel, and a guard of questionable integrity could have any of the keys duplicated for an accomplice.

Better control of the truck keys could be maintained by retaining each set of keys in an individually locked box, furnishing each driver a combination or key that would open only the lockbox holding his own keys.

Occasionally a loss prevention consultant may observe that a loaded trailer has been dropped off at a business or industrial location during the middle of the night. These trailers may contain cargo worth thousands of dollars. There is a possibility of a major theft here, since almost any commercial truck on the road can be used to pull the trailer away. In a theft of this kind, the trailer may be concealed in a distant warehouse or storage area until it can be unloaded and abandoned in another remote area.

The danger of theft may be reduced if the trailer can be left inside a well-fenced, locked yard. A far better arrangement is to leave the trailer inside the truck bay of a locked building. The problem here is that a business does not want to supply a driver with a key that will give him access to a warehouse full of merchandise.

Within recent years new locks have become commercially available to prevent the theft of an entire trailer. These devices are large, weighing about 16 to 17 pounds, and are secured around the kingpin of the trailer in such a way that a truck cannot be hooked onto the trailer. Prior to the availability of these kingpin locks, security men sometimes ran a heavy chain through the wheels of the trailer, padlocking the chain to a structural member. In a number of instances where this arrangement was used, thieves managed to cut the chain and haul the trailer away.

It may also be helpful to paint the company name on the roof of all company trailers in large, easily read letters so that a police helicopter or airplane can quickly spot a stolen trailer being pulled along a roadway.

DRIVER COLLECTIONS

It is frequently necessary for delivery drivers to make cash collections. There are a number of possibilities for loss here.

Many companies have found that it is a questionable procedure to allow drivers to hold collections for more than a day or two. Unless there is regular accountability, some drivers will begin to borrow from the company funds that they are holding. The employee may have every intention of squaring away his accounts, but he could get in too deep before he realizes what has happened.

Then, too, some drivers will hold onto collections for several days and then leave town. In most instances they can be convicted of embezzlement if a criminal charge is filed, but this is often not worth the trouble involved. It can be argued that management asks for this trouble by failing to balance driver accounts on a daily basis.

Robbery represents another potential loss. This can usually be prevented by purchasing a supply of routemen's safes, about 10 inches by 6 inches by 6 inches in size. Some of these safes can be bolted or welded to the metal floor or support inside the truck. Routemen's safes have drop slots for the insertion of money; it is not necessary to give the driver a key.

Many other businesses have found that driver collections will be stolen from the company office unless supervision protects these funds at night. A satisfactory system, for some businesses, requires the driver and supervisor to count receipts together, placing them in a sealed envelope that is dropped into a locked safe equipped with a slot.

Every year some companies regularly report losses varying from a few dollars to $5,000 for a single driver who is not properly supervised or protected.

CONTROLS OVER GASOLINE AND ACCESSORIES

Some companies have made certain that gasoline at the company pump is properly accounted for. This has usually been done by balancing total vehicle usage against the quantity of gasoline pumped into the company tanks. (A small amount of gasoline may, of course, be lost by evaporation.)

Because of the gasoline shortage in recent years, some companies have converted warehouse forklifts and some delivery vehicles to propane fuel. As with gasoline, it is recommended that fuel tanks be adequately secured and that the company use an auditing system to insure that the fuel removed from the tank actually goes into company vehicles.

It can be expected that tires, batteries, and other automobile parts and accessories will be lost unless controls are utilized. If the usage is not great, a simple chain-and-padlock arrangement will usually be adequate to secure tires. It is preferable to store all accessories and supplies in a locked room, however, and to maintain a permanent inventory system. It is also expedient to charge each part or accessory to a specific vehicle and to regularly compare individual unit records with total purchases of automobile and truck items.

FENCES

A good fence may be a requirement in protecting parked trucks and shipping areas. It is the first line of defense against intrusion. This does not mean that a good fence cannot be breached by a determined intruder, and its entire value may be nullified if the gates are not controlled. At best, the fence will only supplement other protective devices and procedures.

In addition, a physical barrier of this kind facilitates the use of designated doorways for the control of traffic, effectively regulating the flow of vehicles and personnel.

A chain-link fence has some security advantages over a stone wall or a wooden fence. Chain-link fencing allows easy observation of the enclosed areas by management, company guards, cruising law enforce-ment officers, or observant passersby. Decorative metal or plastic inserts, placed through the openings in the fence, will cut down on visibility.

Some people object to the institution-like atmosphere that chain-link fencing creates as well as to its failure to hide the industrial aspect of the business. The appearance of the area can be improved consider-ably, however, if stone entryways and decorative steel panels are used for effect at public entries.

In maintaining the security of the fence, it is important that a regular inspection plan be set up to insure that trees and quick-growing weeds do not obstruct visibility.

Physical requirements

In some cities, the municipal code places restrictions on the height of fencing installations, sometimes also regulating whether barbed-wire topping may be used to extend outward or inward from the fence line.

If permitted, an overall height of nine feet is considered a good requirement for security fencing. In the typical installation, this would allow for eight feet of mesh, topped by one foot of tautly strung barbed wire.

It is recommended that the mesh for this fence should be no larger than a two-inch square; otherwise, it would be easy to climb. It is also suggested that the wire should be No. 9 gauge or heavier wire (Ameri-can gauge wire).

All braces for the posts for a fence of this type should be located on the inside of the fence.

The fence should be topped with angled arms or bars, projecting both inward and outward, to create a "V" at an angle of approximately 45 degrees from the perpendicular. Barbed-wire strands should be strung in a taut manner on the angled arms. There should be no less than three strands of wire on each side of the "V." For effective maintenance, the fence should be inspected regularly for indications of illegal entry or evidence of broken or slack strands of barbed wire.

It is recommended that the wire mesh be secured to metal pipe standards, set in concrete. The size of the standards may vary from location to location, but they should be of sufficient size to withstand reasonable contact by vehicles. Experience shows that the hardware that secures the wire mesh to the standards should be bolted, then welded. In many installations, bolts can be removed in a matter of a few minutes by a would-be intruder equipped with a small pair of pliers.

Securing and anchoring the fence

It is extremely difficult to dismantle a chain-link fence or to remove a section of wiring if the bolts have been spot-welded or "peened" so that the bolt threads are flattened at the time the hardware is installed. In addition, all bolts should be inside the fenced enclosure, so that the nuts are difficult to reach.

It is preferable for the wire mesh to be anchored to the ground or secured in the paving at the time of the original installation. This, of course, will prevent intruders from prying the fence upward to provide crawl space under the wire mesh. If not secured originally, weakness may be corrected by fastening the bottom of the fence into a cement curbing. As an alternative, a heavy wire or light cable may be woven through the mesh at the bottom of the installation, with the cable secured tautly.

Fence gates

Fence gates may not be effective unless they are as high as the fence proper, and where feasible the barbed-wire topping on the gate should correspond to the pattern of barbed wire in the fence. If the barbed-wire configuration on top of the gate interferes with opening and closing, it is suggested that the wire extend straight upward rather than be deleted from the top of the gate.

Where possible, the gates should be secured by means of a post-locking arrangement, utilizing a locking bar and latch welded to the gate frame to prevent easy removal and secured with a good-quality padlock. Security of the gate will, of course, be compromised unless keys to the padlock are rigidly controlled and issued to drivers on a need basis.

A double-gate fence opening is usually secured by chaining the two gates together. Frequently, however, an arrangement of this kind gives too much play between the gates, allowing them to be spread apart. If a center-post arrangement can be used, better security can usually be maintained.

Affixing a padlock on a vehicle gate by a chain, welded to the shackle of the padlock, is recommended to prevent removal or substitution of the lock. It is also suggested that the serial numbers from the bottom of gate padlocks be scratched off. Otherwise, the serial number can be copied and used to obtain a duplicate key from an unscrupulous locksmith. If the serial number is removed, it may be helpful to retain a confidential record of the numbers by specific location of the locks. If that is not done, it will be difficult to identify a particular lock, should the need arise.

Yard drains and ditches

It is essential that each ditch or entryway under the fence line be adequately secured at the time of the original installation. To play safe, any opening larger than 96 square inches should be covered with a substantial physical barrier. Ditches or entryways should be covered with steel bars, no less that ⅜ inch in diameter, welded to a steel frame or installed in reinforced concrete or other masonry.

Fence alarms

A number of effective alarm systems are available to alert a central control station or a company guard shack to an attempted breach of a fence. Some of the more effective alarms utilize a laser beam projected along the inside of the fence line. An alarm is set off if someone passes through the invisible laser beam. This system, however, is sometimes expensive to install.

Some other effective fence alarms use a taut-wire arrangement that activates a signal if the tension of the taut wire is either lowered or increased. Pressure against the fence or the weight of an individual on the wire would set off this alarm.

In the past, false alarms have been frequent in some fence-alarm installations; a blowing sheet of newspaper or a wandering dog could set off an unwanted signal. These problems have been effectively reduced in a number of modern alarm systems.

Calling attention to the fence

The effectiveness of a fence will be reduced if approaches to the installation are not in plain view at all times. Accordingly, it is preferable for the entire fence line to be illuminated by a good lighting system.

The psychological effectiveness of a security fence may be enhanced by placing signs on it at regular intervals advising would-be intruders that the enclosed property is private and that anyone who enters illegally will be prosecuted to the full extent of the law. The applicable statute or code section of the law may be added to the signs.

PART
5

CRIMINAL PROBLEMS

Chapter
16

Robbery

THERE IS ALWAYS a possibility that a business may be robbed, especially if large amounts of money are retained on the premises. This type of crime is not limited to supermarkets and small shops, so that management should consider acquainting key employees with some of the problems they may confront.

From time to time, some business people question whether the time and money involved in combating armed robbery are well spent. Most authorities believe that certainty of punishment is the best possible deterrent. If violators are apprehended and brought to trial in a high percentage of these cases, there should be less risk to the safety of business employees, and monetary losses should be considerably reduced.

Management has three basic objectives in contending with this crime: (1) To provide for employee and customer safety, (2) to hold money losses to a minimum, and (3) to furnish police with information that will lead to the identification and apprehension of the individuals responsible.

TWO BASIC TYPES OF BUSINESS ROBBERY

Some students of crime place business robberies into two broad classes: holdups committed by professional criminals who analyze and weigh the risks before becoming involved and holdups committed either by amateurs on an impulse or by irrational individuals, such as drug addicts, who must have money at any cost.

A professional holdup man can usually be expected to balance the risks against the possibilities for obtaining a great deal of money. If it is apparent that he cannot expect much loot, then he will not make the attempt. If he also feels there is a considerable likelihood of failure, the professional will seldom be tempted.

On the other hand, individuals addicted to drugs may become involved in a robbery any time they are short of money. Because of the craving, the addict may ignore logic, even though he or she knows the risks are considerable.

What this means is that a business may protect itself against the professional robber, but can never completely eliminate the possibility of a holdup by irrational amateurs, drug addicts, or impulse criminals. The probability for eliminating professional robberies is usually well worth the effort and cost.

Of course, there are certain types of businesses that are more likely to be held up. Usually these include shops or businesses that remain open during the night hours or that are located in out-of-the-way areas. In general, small food stores, bars and liquor establishments, service stations, and motels are among the businesses that are likely to suffer loss.

EMPLOYEE PLANNING SESSIONS

Some companies run through a simulated robbery. One of the problems here is that some employees could be unduly alarmed. It is therefore suggested that training and instructions be handled in a low-key manner.

Experience seems to indicate that it is helpful to provide instruction cards to key employees, such as tellers, cashiers, or vault-room employees. These cards furnish instructions that can be followed quickly in a time of considerable stress, when the employee may be confused or overwhelmed by the events that have just taken place.

One of these instruction cards can be carried in an employee's purse or billfold, or retained in a desk drawer. As a precaution, the card should not be located in the same drawer in which currency is retained, as there is always a possibility that it could be scooped up and carried away by the thief. Some businesses have found it practical to reduce the size of the instruction card on a duplicating machine that has reduction capacity. A typical instruction card reads as follows:

1. Put up no resistance that will harm yourself or bystanders.
2. Trip the silent alarm.
3. Set off surveillance camera.
4. Make sure "marked money" is given to thief.
5. Form mental picture of thief—description, dress, appearance, peculiarities.
6. Call police, whether or not an alarm was sent. Telephone number _____.
7. Protect any evidence left, dropped, touched by the thief.
8. Note how getaway was made—observe car license if possible.
9. Jot down names and addresses of everybody who was present or who may be a witness.
10. Give paper to witnesses so they can write down descriptions and so forth.
11. Post someone at door to let police know thief has left.
12. Keep curious out; notify company auditor.

In general, the instructions given by the holdup man should be followed as carefully as possible. Clerks and cashiers should be taught to react methodically and deliberately. Even though the employee of the business may be able to protect himself, there is still the possibility that a customer could be seriously injured or killed.

News accounts frequently play up the fact that a store owner or employee had the audacity to engage in a scuffle with an armed robber and succeeded in disarming and overpowering the criminal. Instances of this kind make good headlines but may expose employees and customers to serious harm. Employees should therefore seldom be encouraged to resist.

REDUCING THE LIKELIHOOD OF ROBBERY

Management can take additional steps to reduce the likelihood of a holdup. In a retail store, for example, checkers and cashiers should not be permitted to balance their own cash in locations where their activities can be easily observed by passersby.

One effective precaution is to insure that at least two employees are present when the business facility is closed. This seems to reduce the likelihood that a lone employee will be robbed as soon as other employees have left the premises.

Another good precaution is to require tellers to keep cash register drawers closed after each transaction, as some bandits state that they were tempted because the drawer seemed to be open most of the time.

A number of mechanical aids may prove helpful in reducing the likelihood of robbery. Surveillance (movie) cameras and closed circuit TV sets (CCTV) are frequently helpful in enabling security officers to observe a holdup in progress or to take photographs that help in identifying the subject at a later date. Surveillance cameras and closed circuit TV sets are also very helpful psychological deterrents. In general, however, surveillance cameras and CCTV installations are expensive and may not be justified in small businesses or in small branch locations. TV circuits are ineffective unless the monitor is observed almost constantly. This is an excellent precaution in many locations, but the cost is a definite factor.

INFORM THE POLICE OF "CASING"

Most professional holdups occur only after observation and study of the premises and the habits of employees. This "casing" activity may take many guises, but it is frequently recognizable when the employees of the business are alert to it.

The habits and activity patterns of most customers in a retail business are very predictable. At times a "customer" may simply seem to be out of place. A sixth sense may alert the store clerk to the possibility that the individual on the other side of the counter may not really be a customer. Store employees should not spend any great amount of time in attempting to detect persons "casing" the business for a robbery. However, clerks should not lose sight of the fact that this may be a possibility, especially if the store is one that carries expensive jewelry or other merchandise, or if large sums of money are accumulated in the business.

When an employee suspects that a person has been casing a retail or wholesale establishment, it may be desirable to notify the manager or supervisor by some type of a prearranged signal that is not observable to anyone else. If such a signal is received, it may be possible for the management representative to walk out of the building and observe the license plates of any suspicious automobiles parked nearby. This does not mean that employees should play detective but that they should remain alert and act accordingly.

If robbery seems to be a distinct possibility, management should consider hiring a uniformed, armed guard. This may be in addition to a silent system. In some instances the guard may function as a helpful public relations contact for employees, while serving both as a psychological and an active deterrent to business robbery.

HOLDING DOWN THE LOSS

A common-sense policy for minimizing the amount of money on hand is an effective method to prevent loss or to minimize loss in the event of a robbery.

It is usually helpful to set a money limit, and to require the cashier or teller to take money to the bank whenever that limit is exceeded. One of the problems here is that the messenger may be held up while carrying funds to the bank. If possible, the company should use the services of an armored car or send a uniformed, armed guard with the person transporting the funds.

Regardless of attempts to keep operating routines on a confidential basis, it is frequently known in the community if a company allows money to build up. Some businesses restrict the amount of cash that is accessible to employees after most other businesses have closed for the night. Drop chutes may be built into safes for the use of routemen or deliverymen who bring in substantial amounts of money late in the day. Additional physical protection and armed guards may be justified if it is necessary to retain substantial amounts of cash on hand.

Police officials in almost every city can cite cases in which holdup men were encouraged by seeing large amounts of money carelessly stuffed into a cash register. Cash registers should be "bled" frequently and the funds taken from the registers should be placed into a protected, alarmed money room that is kept locked at all times.

If it is necessary for an employee or member of management to carry money to the bank, it is suggetsed that the cloth bank bag not be carried openly. It is preferable to place the bank bag in a paper sack or a brief case so that it is not so noticeable.

An armored car service should be used where the cost can be justified. Company funds, however, should not be turned over to anyone wearing an armored car service uniform unless this individual is known on sight or can properly identify himself. Police records reflect a number of instances in which persons posing as armored car service guards have picked up large amounts of money when in fact those individuals in uniform were impostors.

When salesmen are required to collect considerable quantities of cash during the day, it may be desirable to make some provision for protecting these funds. This is usually accomplished by welding or bolting a locked, fabricated steel box to the frame of the company vehicle. If the driver is not furnished a key to the box, it is unlikely that he will be asked to open it. Commercially available steel safes, of small size, can be used for this purpose.

KIDNAPPING THE STORE MANAGER

It is not unusual for holdup men to kidnap a store manager. In most cases of this kind, the criminals may force their way into the manager's home after claiming to be police officers or pretending to need access to a telephone because of an emergency. Once inside, these individuals may draw guns and force the manager to accompany one of them to open the store safe. Meanwhile, another bandit will remain with the manager's family, keeping them under control at the point of a gun. Upon receiving a signal that the manager has opened the safe, the bandit at the home will make his getaway.

Not all crimes of this type can be avoided. However, if management officials are alert to this possibility, they may be able to take precautions to prevent criminals from getting into their homes.

As additional protection, some modern safes have two combinations, either of which will open the safe on the robber's command. One of the combinations, however, will activate an alarm in a central alarm station, alerting the alarm company to the fact that a robbery is in progress. Safes with time-lock arrangements are also available, making it impossible for anyone to open the safe during nighttime hours.

THE COMPANY MONEY ROOM

Many security consultants recommend that the company's money room be located in an inner room, where any traffic involving non-employees is readily apparent. Other security consultants believe that the company funds should be located where activity may be within public observation. In either event, it is desirable to use a locked door with a peep hole as well as an alarm button inside the money room proper.

PROTECTING CHECKS AND OTHER NEGOTIABLES

In their haste to obtain whatever is available, holdup men frequently grab checks and negotiables along with currency. In most instances thieves will never attempt to cash stolen checks; however, this possibility should never be ruled out. If checks are stamped "For Deposit Only" at the time of receipt, they cannot be negotiated.

ROBBERY AT OPENING OR CLOSING TIME

Holdup men have long been aware that they may have more control over their victims by robbing a business when customers are not present. This, of course, is usually at opening or closing time.

If a lone employee usually remains on the premises for some time before another employee reports for duty, there is increased vulnerability. Thus some companies follow a policy of requiring a two-employee opening. There is always a possiblity that a criminal may have broken into the building during the night, intending to confront employees after they enter. The usual technique here is for the bandit to step out of a hiding place with a gun and force an employee to open a locked safe or money drawer. In many cases the holdup man can remain in the building with a mask over his features, making identification very difficult later. If the first employees who enter are unable to open the safe, the bandit may tie them up or force them into a closet until the arrival of the employee with the combination.

If the business is vulnerable to this kind of attack, one employee should open the premises while another remains outside. If there is no one hiding in the building, the individual checking the premises can give a signal to the employee waiting outside. In the event the prearranged signal is not given, the employee on the outside should immediately go to a telephone and call the police.

SETTING OFF THE ALARM

If it is possible for an employee to set off a silent holdup alarm, that type of alarm should be installed. Similarly, it is very desirable to have a camera-surveillance system that the employee can activate inconspicuously. If the employee cannot set off the silent alarm without being obvious, then the employee must consider his or her personal safety first and set off the alarm as the thief walks out the door—or even a minute or two later to be absolutely safe.

An alarm system that the bandit can hear is of questionable value; he may panic and discharge a weapon at anyone in his path.

SUMMONING THE POLICE

Employees should realize that if an alarm can be transmitted to the police, there is always a good possibility of an apprehension while the bandit is in flight. It should not be assumed that the police will respond immediately after an alarm signal has been sent. Most alarm installations function properly, but there could be a delay or a mechanical malfunction.

A telephone call to the police will enable the police dispatcher to ask hurried, pertinent questions while the caller is on the line. If the employee making the call will continue to keep the line open, the dispatcher will frequently be able to ask questions that may be of considerable significance while the holdup is in progress. Time, of course, is of the essence.

The police telephone number should be posted where it is instantly available, and employees should be informed that their first call should be to the police station rather than to a company executive or auditor.

Some companies have successfully worked out systems for employees to give a prearranged robbery signal to a co-worker. But unless employees are alert, this precaution may be useless. Many instances are on file, however, of holdup attempts that have been broken up by this kind of employee action.

HELPING THE POLICE IDENTIFY THE CRIMINAL

If all businesses follow a policy of working closely with police officers, the robbery rate may fall off considerably. Obtaining and recording an accurate physical description of the holdup man is often crucial. Attention should be given to any peculiarities or unusual features, or distinctive aspects of the bandit's dress. Some businesses, especially those that handle considerable amounts of money, provide employees with a preprinted form for recording the holdup person's physical characteristics. If a system of this kind is not followed, it is suggested that management immediately provide a pencil and blank paper for each employee who was a possible witness. These individuals should record descriptive information without consultation among themselves, as the independent impressions of the witnesses are usually more accurate than those that are influenced by others.

PROTECTING EVIDENCE

Witnesses frequently observe that a holdup man touched certain items during the course of the robbery or that he dropped certain objects in his flight. Management should take the responsibility of insuring that anything touched, dropped, or left by the thief is protected until the police arrive. Objects of this kind should not be handled at all, unless necessary. It should be assumed that anything touched or left is potential evidence.

OBSERVING THE GETAWAY

The files of almost every police agency contain cases in which victims and onlookers seemed to freeze during the course of a robbery, failing to note how the getaway was made. There are many other cases on file, however, in which an alert individual was able to observe the license plate number of a getaway car or develop other significant facts about the criminal's flight. Employees should, of course, continue to think of their personal safety at this stage of the crime, but they can frequently obtain information of value without undue exposure.

Another helpful technique may be to assign an employee to immediately record the license plate number of automobiles parked around the business or on nearby parking lots. With this information the police will be able to question individuals who were parked nearby at the time of the robbery. As a practical matter, some police investigators may not have the time to locate and interview the users and occupants of these parked automobiles as potential witnesses. If, however, the crime is an especially serious one, such as armed robbery, this information may be welcome to the police.

PRESS ANNOUNCEMENTS

Some businesses seem to feel that they have an obligation to the public to inform the press of all details of a robbery, burglary, or other crime committed against the business. Usually, authorities on robbery feel that this practice may be unwise. If a news release reflects that a large sum of cash was taken, other criminals may be encouraged to come back for a second robbery. If there are other branches in the business, attacks may be made against these branches. In some cases the facts cannot be kept from the press, but management should withhold any information that would indicate that the business is an easy mark.

Chapter 17

Burglary

STUDIES OVER A NUMBER of years have indicated that burglary is usually a crime of opportunity. Most violations are unsophisticated attacks, directed at homes or businesses that have very little physical protection. Then, too, burglary is frequently a teenager's crime.

This does not mean that there is any shortage of professional criminals in this field. If a business continues to accumulate large sums of money and uses an antiquated money safe or vault, there is considerable risk. Numerically, there are few criminals who have the training and experience to rip out the corner of a safe, punch out the spindle, drill the spindle, or use explosives. Nevertheless, neither type of burglary should be dismissed lightly.

Professional burglaries can best be prevented by installing a good alarm system, protecting doors and windows, using adequate money safes, and in some cases hiring guards. There is not much likelihood that a professional burglar will be tempted if these physical protective devices are obvious and if everyone in the company knows that funds are regularly taken to the bank.

The amateur burglar usually knows from the outset that he cannot get into the money safe, yet he may still break into the premises. Often this kind of burglary is never reported, since the individual loss may be very small.

One authority on business security problems described the motivation and activities of an amateur burglar as follows:

The person feels a need. He sees an opportunity for a burglary and rationalizes that the crime will be a way to fill this need. He commits the crime and gets away without detection. Proceeds from the crime are then converted to money or otherwise exchanged for ego-pleasing items. Because the burglar's need seems satisfied, the behavior is reinforced. The whole chain of events seems justified in the burglar's mind, and it is quite likely to be repeated.

Three basic approaches can be recommended to business to reduce the likelihood of any kind of burglary. These are:

1. Force the criminal to spend considerable time to get in or to remove anything of value from the business;
2. Reduce the available loot in both money and merchandise; and
3. Make it physically difficult or dangerous to get in.

THE TIME FACTOR

Almost invariably, burglars, armed robbers, and other criminals have an aversion to time delays. The longer the wrongdoer is involved at the scene, the greater the likelihood that he will be apprehended there. Any thinking criminal knows that he may have tripped an unseen alarm device as he entered or that his entry into the premises may have been observed by someone in the neighborhood. Then, too, if police or armed guard patrols are made with reasonable frequency, it may be only a matter of time until the entry is detected.

In planning warehouse and stockroom location, it is usually desirable to retain expensive merchandise in locations that may be difficult to reach. If a thief must spend considerable time in transporting merchandise to an open door or window, there is greater likelihood that he may be caught while still in the building.

There are two basic types of safes that are used by businesses: fire safes and money safes. The former type offers good protection to company records in the event of a fire. Some companies, especially small businesses, do not feel that they can justify the expense to buy safes that protect against both fire and burglary. As a result, many businesses still use a fire safe for the storage of both company books and funds.

An experienced burglar with proper tools can quickly rip open almost any fire safe. Because of the time element, the burglar may prefer to attack a safe of this kind rather than to be exposed for hours in attempting to loot a business money safe, where success may be problematic.

REDUCING THE LOOT AVAILABLE

It was emphasized earlier that large sums of money should not be allowed to accumulate on the premises. Petty cash should be retained in the company safe overnight and in a locked desk drawer or locked safe during the daytime. Postage stamps, coffee funds, and vending machine money will sometimes attract dishonest individuals.

In the absence of available money, burglars may remove typewriters, electric calculators, adding machines, or company merchandise. If the company product or merchandise is easily salable, it may be the primary target. Items such as jewelry, watches, and merchandise of unusual value should be afforded additional protection. If an alarm system does not seem justified for the entire warehouse, an alarm covering a special area should be considered.

Police departments regularly recover merchandise, machines, typewriters, and the like from burglars; however, detectives are frequently unable to identify the place where the loot was taken from. Consequently, all businesses should maintain an inventory of mechanical equipment, typewriters, business machines, guns, and similar items by serial number. As mentioned before, many police departments now sponsor programs to loan electric tool engravers or markers to businesses so that identifying marks can be placed on property. If the criminal knows that property is marked, he may realize it is unwise to become involved in a burglary at this particular establishment.

Physical or mechanical preventive devices

Providing good physical and mechanical protection for a business building is sometimes described as "hardening the target" by police authorities.

Given unlimited time and equipment, many burglars would eventually break into a well-protected building. But if store windows, skylights, doors, and other entryways are adequately protected, it is usually quite difficult to get in. Good locks and hardware are needed, and heavy steel mesh or steel bars should be welded to windows or other openings that are not within easy view of the public and police patrols.

It is advisable to consider the probability of burglary prior to the construction of a business building. Eliminating unnecessary windows or openings and placing entryways in full view of the street will automatically eliminate many of the possibilities of attack. The use of uniformed guards should also be considered in the planning stage.

Some installations use alarm systems around the perimeter only, on the theory that the burglar must break through the perimeter or outer shell of the building to gain entrance. Although systems of this kind are usually effective, it is always possible that the burglar may have hidden out in the building prior to closing time or that he might break through a vent shaft or skylight that is not covered by the system. Other, more sophisticated burglary systems use sonic motion detection, radio-frequency detection, or other principles that will send an alarm if a burglar enters a particular section where high-value merchandise is stored.

Management should obtain some knowledge of burglary alarm systems prior to approving an installation. Costs vary considerably, and needs differ widely from business to business. These considerations should be reviewed only with an informed representative of a legitimate alarm company.

The advantages of a silent alarm are usually much greater than those of an audible or local alarm. Unless someone goes to the trouble to call the police department when an audible alarm rings, there may never be any police response. Then, too, an audible alarm lets the burglar know that he has been detected, so he can immediately flee.

Chapter 18

Control of movement of employees, visitors, and vendors

MANY COMPANIES, especially those with a number of employees and those situated in densely populated areas, may want to bolster their security measures by establishing an employee identification system. Most identification systems use cards or badges. The advantages of such systems are numerous and permit great flexibility. Not only do they provide quick, accurate identification of employees, but they can also be used for restricting access to specific areas and for spotting intruders or visitors who may have lost their way.

A number of commercially available identification card- and badge-making units can produce a usable employee card or badge within a few minutes, at a minimum of cost. In considering a system of this kind, it may be desirable to design the identification card so that it can be punched for insertion of a clip or other device that will enable it to be used as a badge on the employee's clothing.

The information that should be included on an identification card will vary with the needs of the particular business. It is important, however, for the identification of the bearer to be made almost instantly, and it is very helpful if the badge is color-coded in such a distinctive manner that it will be apparent if the wearer is in an area without authority. Security guards, fencing, lighting, electronic equipment, and locking devices may not be effective unless the badge system is used and adequately controlled.

PRINCIPLES AND PROCEDURES
FOR IDENTIFICATION BADGES

At the minimum, the badge should have the following information imprinted on it:

1. Employee's photograph.
2. Physical description (possibly on back of badge).
3. Authorizing signature.
4. Employee number.
5. Date of issue.
6. Place of assignment (by symbol or color).
7. Employee's signature and/or employee's thumbprint.

Experience indicates that facilities should be available to produce the badge as soon after hire as possible. If there is any delay in producing the photographic badge, a controlled temporary badge should be issued. Temporary badge controls should include numerical-sequence control in clearly visible location, expiration-date stamp, and full accountability of each temporary badge issued. The system should require the employee to turn in the temporary badge when the permanent badge is issued.

Color codes should be so prominent that they are readily distinguishable. One distinctive color can be used for members of management who have complete access, and other colors used for sensitive or restricted areas of the business, such as the computer room.

Whenever an identification badge is reported lost or stolen, a system should be used to disseminate this information to each point of entry into the plant, facility, or business. This "hot sheet" system is essential to prevent the use of unauthorized badges and to recover identification badges if an illegal penetration should be attempted. This list should include terminee identification badges not returned at the time of separation.

Employees sometimes forget to bring their badges to work. In that event, it is suggested that a temporary badge, with a one-day expiration date imprinted on it, be issued. The "T," or temporary, badge would be issued by the guard at the lobby to an employee who lost or forgot his permanent badge. This would be issued only after verification of employment with the worker's supervisor. Badges would be controlled by the number at the bottom. The badge would be retrieved by the guard at the time of departure, at the point of issuance only. This would require the employee to depart through the place where he entered. The guard would log the name and compare it with the card number issued for that name. Any cards not turned in at the end of the day would be recovered at the start of the next day.

Identification cards can be constructed to avoid easy duplication. A distinctive type of card stock, imprinted with an unusual logo or company symbol, may be helpful. Unissued card stock may be sequentially numbered and kept secured when not in use. A company seal or other distinctive device may also be impregnated on the card stock when it is laminated.

The identification system will not be effective, however, unless supervisors and employees are encouraged to immediately report individuals who are in a restricted area or who appear to be using an unauthorized card.

It is also recommended that the company keep a record of each card by employee name, date, identification card number, and date of destruction after being returned. As a continuation of this program, all badges should be reissued periodically for updating purposes and for insuring their effectiveness for continued use.

ACCESS CONTROLS

There are many systems for maintaining access controls to buildings. Experience shows that guards frequently grant entry into a company building on the basis of visual recognition alone. This is objectionable for a number of reasons. The guard may make a mistaken identification—the individual seeking admittance may have been fired a few days earlier—or the guard may be unable to recall whom he admitted after the lapse of a short time. It is therefore important to maintain a record of persons entering and departing and to make certain that the record is accurate.

Card-key control systems, associated with a minicomputer, can provide a high level of control. These systems can be used to deny access to an employee who has been fired, but to allow entry to a proper cardholder. Distinct advantages of such a system are:

1. Eliminates the necessity for keys to external doors.
2. Does away with the need for manpower to unlock or lock remote doors.
3. Allows doors to be operated from great distances and maintains control over a number of doors, as needed.

4. Provides a record of the card used to lock, unlock, or give status identification at each door.

If it is necessary to keep out persons who have been fired, the system will reject cards issued to these individuals. One of the weaknesses of this system is that an unauthorized person could steal or borrow a card issued to someone else. To eliminate unauthorized entry, a guard can visually inspect the photograph laminated inside an identification card of this kind. If the card is then inserted into the system card reader, the access door will open only if the card is still valid.

CONTROL OF VENDORS, SUPPLIERS, AND DELIVERYMEN

Most companies have no authority over vendor representatives sent to handle deliveries or contractual obligations. Control over the entry, exit, and activities of these individuals inside the business establishment is essential to security.

An access-procedure program for deliverymen and outside sales representatives should include a single gate or entryway for ingress and exit, numerical control over vendor passes issued at the point of entry, and a list of vendors and delivery representatives, along with a list of persons authorized to represent each of these companies. The list should be made available at the control gate.

The program should also include a written record of the number of the badge issued, along with the date of issue, name of vendor or supplier, signature of vendor's representative, license number of delivery vehicle, destination in the building, time in and time out, and signature of security officer or guard on duty. A record should be made of the invoice number and freight or air bill number represented by the delivery. This should include a description of the property in a few words and a record of the number of pieces to be delivered. If the entire load on a delivery is not to be taken off, action should be taken to determine the total number of pieces aboard at the time of departure so that a verification can be made. Rules and regulations for nonemployees making deliveries or coming onto the premises should be posted, and there should be a procedure for inspecting the delivery vehicle, according to need, at the time of entry and departure.

It is suggested that permanent vendor passes be issued only when an adequate system is in effect to retrieve passes and when expiration dates are considered and passes picked up.

VISITORS' PASSES

A visitor is usually easier to control than employees or vendors' representatives. In most circumstances, the visitor will have an appointment with some official of the business, or be granted an appointment, prior to being given access. Figure 6 shows a typical visitor's pass. It is suggested that the visitor-pass procedure include the following:

The receptionist or guard on duty should be notified in advance

Figure 6. A typical visitor's pass.

```
┌────────────────────────────────────────────────────┐
│              XYZ Ship Lines                          │
│              VISITOR'S PASS                          │
│  Expires: _____   │
│  First name: _____ Last: _____   │
│  Person to visit: _____   │
│  Visitor's company or organization: _____   │
│  _____   │
│ - - - - - - - - - - - - - - - - - - - - - - - - - -  │
│  Purpose of visit: _____   │
│  Visitor's signature: _____   │
│  Escort's signature and section: _____   │
│  _____   │
│  Date issued: _____   │
│  Building entrance: _____   │
│  Time in:                     AM _____   │
│                               PM _____   │
│  Time out:                    AM _____   │
│                               PM _____   │
│  Guard issuing: _____   │
└────────────────────────────────────────────────────┘
```

A duplicate of this two-part form is given to the visitor. The top part is the size of a credit card and can be inserted into a plastic badge holder and attached to the visitor's outer clothing. The bottom part is retained by the security guard or receptionist who issues the pass.

that a visitor is expected. The time of the visitor's appointment should be given, along with the entryway he or she is expected to use. A log should be maintained recording the visitor's name and company, the official with whom he or she has an appointment, time of entry, badge number issued, and time out. A carbon copy of the badge issued may be used as a control to insure that the visitor left the building as expected.

The receptionist or guard should announce each visitor who has an appointment. If the outsider arrives without an appointment, access should not be granted until approval is obtained from the company official whom this individual is to see.

LOCK AND KEY SYSTEMS

Systems to control and audit locks and keys are of definite importance in a loss prevention program. As in other areas of business, good security requires a wise selection of locks, followed by a responsible program for making changes consistent with needs, cost, and practicality. No lock is more secure than the manner in which it is installed, nor is it any more secure than the combination or the keys that operate it. It is difficult to set a price on the cost of periodic precautionary rekeying, compared with the cost of external losses that may occur without leaving visible signs of entry into the building.

Many businesses have found that sound lock and key control practices make it a necessity to have a qualified locksmith on their payroll or under contract for regular service.

Minimizing the number of keys

The first principle in an effective system is to minimize the number of keys to a business building that are given out. Too often, keys are issued solely for prestige or convenience. At one Los Angeles business occupying less than half a square block in size a loss prevention consultant recently found that 32 keys to the front were outstanding. The business was a family-owned corporation operated by three brothers. Each of the brothers, sons, nephews, and cousins in the family carried a door key to maintain their sense of importance. In addition, two supervisors who were not members of the family held keys because of job necessity.

Not only must key control be applied stringently, it must be applied continuously. Most keyholders do not stop to realize that a key may be duplicated in a matter of minutes and that this loss of accountability may be a distinct possibility anytime a key is loaned overnight or even for a short time. It is therefore important for key-holders to be advised at the outset that they must have the key in their immediate possession at all times.

In one recent case in Tampa, Florida, a dishonest employee duplicated a key when he was supposedly on a coffee break. The warehouse superintendent had thrown his ring of door keys to the employee in question, ordering the back warehouse door to be unlocked. Needless to add, the warehouse was burglarized the next night.

Fixing responsibility for keys

In a very small company it may be possible for one individual to remember which employees have been furnished keys. But "record keeping" by memory is not recommended. Instead, records should be kept, by lock or by secured area, of all keys issued to individual employees. When the security requirements of a department or area change, the record should be revised and indicated changes made.

If an employee is terminated or reassigned to new duties, it is also suggested that his file be reviewed to determine his continuing need for keys.

Still another problem stems from the fact that keys should be identifiable to management by number without revealing to unauthorized individuals which particular doors or locks the key will activate.

The key cabinet itself should be a high-security area and should not be accessible to unauthorized individuals.

Regular key audits

Periodic key audits are a vital part of control. The employee to whom the key is assigned should be asked to physically produce it, and the key should then be tested to make certain that there has not been a substitution. Sometimes it will be found that keys to high-security areas have been mislaid, loaned, or lost, and the employee may have been hesitant to report it. In addition, a physical audit may reveal that the key is being maintained in an unsafe location, so that other individuals have access to it. (Of course, management is never completely sure that an employee has not knowingly or unknowingly permitted another individual to have an unauthorized copy made.)

Some companies have found it practical to have special key blanks with the company name on the bow, as well as with the notation "do not duplicate." If the company's own blank is used, management can immediately realize from an audit that an unauthorized duplication has been made.

Periodic replacement and re-keying

With time, locks wear out and need to be replaced. Yet it is common for the old cylinders to continue to be used. However, replacing entire locks is expensive. An effective alternative is to install locks with removable cores. Some retail stores have found that cores can be removed and stored for a year or two and then used as replacements. Usually, they are put back into service at a different installation or different store, without re-keying. This is not recommended, however, if an employee who carried the key has been dismissed from the company.

A practical worksheet used to give positive accountability for all keys issued is shown in Figure 7.

Figure 7. Key holder survey worksheet.

		Keys Currently in Employees' Possession																
Building or Floor No. North Warehouse																		
					Door or Room Numbers													
		Receiving Door	Shipping Door #1	Shipping Door #2	Shipping Door #3	Shipping Door #4	Rear Dock Door	Spice Room	Railroad Siding	Electrical Panels	Freezer #1	Dangerous Chemical	Boiler Room					
Name	Position																	Need for Key
J. T. Wilkin	Whse. Supt.	X	X	X	X	X	X				X							To open up
Al Stoner	Chemist							X		X								Access to chemicals

Customer problems

SHOPLIFTING

NOTHING CAN BE more frustrating than for a manager to believe that he has the formula for making a profit in today's competitive market, only to see that profit dissipated through ineffective loss prevention controls. Employee theft is undoubtedly the major part of the problem here, but customer losses are also significant.

In some respects it may be easier for management to formulate controls for employees than for customers. In the first place, the workforce of a store is relatively small compared with the great number of customers who pour through the doors of the average business. It is also worth noting that management may have almost continuous contacts with employees, while customer contacts last for only a short time, and may be repeated on only a few occasions.

In addition, management can force controls on employees. Company regulations concerning refunds, receiving procedures, cash handling, employee purchases, and other specific subjects can be spelled out, and management can insist on compliance with those rules.

No company will remain in business very long if customer relations are completely ignored. Merchandising attitudes have developed through experience, and some companies feel that it may be a mistake to force management controls on the general public. The thinking here is that the legitimate customer should simply not be asked to submit to controls. Some authorities on merchandising believe that traffic-flow barriers, forcing customers to exit through a check-stand gate, may be objectionable to some shoppers. Others feel that prominent signs, warning of the penalty for shoplifting, may also be offensive to a legitimate customer. Nevertheless, there is a definite need for customer controls, and management seeks a delicate balance between offending the honest customer and keeping losses within practical limits.

The type of merchandise on the shelves of a retail store has a direct bearing on the extent of inventory shortages that may be anticipated unless good security is maintained. Merchandise that has strong buyer appeal and items that are easy to resell are principal targets. Junior dresses, sporting goods, sportswear, small leather goods, young men's clothing, costume and genuine jewelry, watches, cameras, cosmetics, and phonograph records are among the items that are particularly attractive to shoplifters.

Proof of shoplifting

Under U.S. criminal law, guilt or innocence usually hinges on whether the accused intended to steal. Before a customer can be found guilty of shoplifting, it is necessary to prove that the person did, in fact, intend to steal. The problem here is that no one really knows what goes on in another person's mind. Since the judge and jury cannot read the thoughts of the accused, the law says that we must decide his intentions from his outward manifestations. Whether the accused seemed to be waiting around until the clerks had no time to observe him, what the accused said, whether he went to pains to conceal the store's merchandise, his other activities in the light of the surrounding circumstances—all these are indicators as to whether the accused had the mental intent to steal.

Absentmindedness is not a crime, and it is not a violation to forget to pay for merchandise. Neither is it a crime in itself to conceal merchandise, but it is an indication of an intent to steal.

From a legal standpoint, an arrest for shoplifting can be made anytime after the suspect's intent has been made clear. Many business people feel that an apprehension cannot be made inside the store but must take place outside. That is not true, in the absence of some unusual local law. As a matter of policy, however, most stores feel that an arrest should not take place until the suspect has gone past the check stand and has gone out of the building, making it quite obvious that the shoplifter never had any intention to pay.

Arresting the shoplifter

The decision to arrest should be restricted to only a few individuals. The manager, or someone designated by him or her, should make the decision, since a lawsuit for false arrest may follow if a mistake is made.

Basically, any person who observes a shoplifting violation (a misdemeanor) has the legal authority to make an arrest. It should be emphasized here that only the person who actually sees the crime committed can make the arrest. As a practical matter, the management official must rely on the judgment of the employee who made the observation. It is then up to the management official to accompany the employee who effects the apprehension.

For an arrest of this kind to be proper, it is essential to observe the shoplifter take the merchandise and conceal it on his person or among his belongings. The criminal must then be kept under observation continuously, or the arrest will not be valid. The person observing all this must be able to testify in court that the accused left without paying for the merchandise, thus indicating an intention to steal. It is not enough to see the merchandise concealed and to then ask the person handling the cash register if it was ever paid for.

The arrest should be made politely but firmly. It is seldom advisable for female store employees to attempt an arrest without a male present, as a fight may ensue when it is apparent that there is no male to assist.

Experience shows that it is usually best to have the manager ask the shoplifter to return to the store to straighten out the problem. If the shoplifter refuses to return or attempts to break away, reasonable force may be used to restrain him or her until the police arrive to take the accused thief into custody.

If the thief does manage to break away, the police should be called immediately and the license number of the automobile furnished to authorities.

If two or more store employees are present and the approach is positive in nature, the shoplifter will usually return to the store. Care should be exercised here in making sure that the criminal is not allowed to get rid of the stolen articles. When the stolen merchandise is surrendered or taken from the shoplifter, it should be held as evidence for the police, along with all boxes, wrappings, blister packs, and price tags that might have been discarded. Price tags of perishable items should be retained. The employee who recovers them should place the date, initials, and name of the apprehended shoplifter on each item of merchandise.

When a policeman arrives to pick up the shoplifter, the officer should be asked to initial and date each item of evidence. He should also be requested to accept the evidence at the time he transports the prisoner.

In some instances the police will refuse to accept this kind of evidence. If that happens, the material should be placed into a sealed container after being identified by initials, by date, and by the name of the shoplifter. Then the package should be taken to court in the event the matter goes to trial.

When the police take the shoplifter into custody, the prosecutor issues a criminal complaint, which must be signed by the store employee who actually made the arrest. This part of the procedure is crucial, since the matter will be dropped unless the complaint is signed. It is also important to note that if a complaint is not filed, the shoplifter may press a civil suit for false arrest and may recover a considerable amount of money from the business.

Some employees show considerable initiative in an investigation of this type, and their interest is commendable. Appropriate caution is recommended, however, to make certain that they do not develop a "detective complex" in handling their regular work.

Employee training

The starting point in combating shoplifting is in training and communicating with employees. One overriding idea should be stressed: A shoplifter seldom steals from the store where there is close customer attention. A legitimate customer never resents helpful service, and a shoplifter never has an opportunity to steal.

Employees should be taught to avoid building blind spots in store displays. Special attention should be given to high display racks that could hide the activities of shoppers.

Clerks should be taught to be suspicious of the customer who insists on small talk while a companion examines merchandise in another area. Clerks should also give careful attention to single customers who seem to browse overly long.

Easily concealed, expensive merchandise should be locked up or controlled in easy view of responsible employees, who have instructions to monitor the merchandise.

A policy should be followed of stapling or sealing packages to prevent the insertion of additional merchandise in another department.

Cash registers should be located near the exits of the store, so that customers must pass by before making their exit and so that one cashier can observe the activities of another to avoid collusion with a dishonest customer. It is also helpful to have a member of management "run the front line."

Clerical workers should also learn to be wary of customers who appear to be drunk, pocketing small items as they reel against a display case. A similar technique used by some shoplifters is to deliberately trip or stumble and grab the counter.

It may also be advisable for management to alert salespeople to some of the shoplifting tricks that are distinctive to a particular type of business. For example, a customer may come into a ladies' clothing store and ask to see an expensive bra. The customer goes into a dressing room and puts on the new bra, intending to wear it home. She then places the old, worn-out bra into the merchandise box and returns it to the sales clerk with a statement to the effect that it is not what she wants. Unless the employee is alert to this ruse, the substitution may not be discovered. If challenged, the customer claims that she forgot she was still wearing the new article and immediately changes it.

Another possibility here is that the box containing the substituted brassiere may be given to a legitimate customer as good merchandise. Arriving home, the purchaser may be quite angry to discover the substituted garment in her box. If she encounters resistance in obtaining a replacement, the customer may be lost.

Other problems, distinctive to a particular type of store or business, should be explained to sales personnel. In a ladies' dress shop, for example, it may be desirable to limit the number of garments that may be taken into a dressing room at one time. If there is no accountability, the customer may slip a new garment on and then cover it by putting her street dress over the store dress. She then walks from the store, "double-dressed."

Clerks should also be taught to examine dressing rooms for price tags that could have been removed from new merchandise as well as other ruses that may be used.

It is also suggested that cash register employees be trained to detect ticket switching. They should also be briefed as to the tactics of short-change artists.

Advertising the security program

Some businesses keep their security staff a secret. In all likelihood, this may increase the number of apprehensions made for shoplifting. This is contrary to accepted loss prevention principles, as it is usually better to keep shoplifters out of the store altogether.

A number of larger stores or store chains have learned that advertising security precautions is very effective in controlling inventory shrinkage. The security directors of these stores believe that the best insurance against theft is an alert, customer-oriented salesperson. They also believe that it pays to advertise the fact that the company has a sophisticated security force. This is done by letting the general public see the closed-circuit TV monitoring room, where the consoles are observed at all times.

In other large stores employees wear jackets with a security emblem on the front. This approach gives the potential shoplifter the impression that an employee always has him in view.

Managers in some retail stores have found it helpful to give the impression that there is considerable activity on the part of security personnel. One store consistently uses loud speakers to call "Security to Area Two" on a half-hour or 45-minute basis. This has been used as a psychological deterrent against shoplifting since a shoplifter may not know where "Area Two" is located.

TICKET SWITCHING

Most price-tag switching used to be done in five-and-dime stores or in clothing establishments. Now it happens in grocery stores and almost every kind of retail establishment. Perhaps because of increased grocery prices, it is not uncommon for a five-pound roast to arrive at the check stand with a tag marked three pounds.

This kind of larceny is difficult to detect and is seldom prosecuted. In most states there is no criminal provision against tampering with merchandise tickets. Generally the violator can be arrested only if he is observed actually changing the ticket, buying the item, and taking it off the premises.

Usually the customer maintains, "I found it just the way it was." There always is the possibility that the mistake was made by the clerk who affixed the tags.

Some tickets are designed to prevent ticket switching. The so-called breakaway ticket or tear-away ticket will shred into small pieces if removed. It can be applied once only. These tickets are effective, but they are slightly more expensive than regular price tags.

For a number of years, manufacturers of security equipment have marketed electronic tickets or tags that will cause a buzzer to ring if a tagged item is carried past a detector located at the check stand. One of the problems here is that the employee at the cash register must remember to remove the tag when the merchandise is wrapped. If this is not done, an alarm sounds, and the manager or security personnel may seriously alienate a customer who is not aware of the sensing device. The usual practice is to place electronic tickets of this kind only on merchandise that is easy to conceal and that represents considerable value.

One potential problem is that a dishonest employee may remove an electronic ticket from an item he wishes to steal and carry the merchandise past the detecting device.

In some stores, management has found that the best solution to ticket switching is to pay a bonus to cashiers who detect such instances. Some employees seem to be quite adept at this art. One effective technique is to double-mark merchandise, placing a tag on the box and an ink stamp on the item it contains.

Another common trick practiced by dishonest customers is switching caps on merchandise when the price has been stamped on them. This type of loss is best controlled by not marking prices on the top of the jar.

TILL TAPPING

"Till tappers" are professional criminals who make their living by removing money from the cash register. Although they do not operate in great numbers, thieves of this class may be responsible for more cash register shortages than is realized.

Till tappers usually work in pairs, making a small purchase or requesting change in order to get the cash register opened. At that moment, the thief at the cash register will divert the clerk's attention, while the accomplice reaches into the cash drawer and removes the bills.

Usually this kind of theft is directed at cash registers that are within easy reach. One of the commonly used techniques is to ask for merchandise displayed behind the counter to get the cashier to turn away from the open cash drawer long enough for the thief to obtain the currency.

Another technique is to drop money or merchandise on the floor, hoping that the register clerk will bend down to pick up the fallen object. When the clerk rises, the drawer may be empty of bills.

If the register clerks are taught to complete each sale before going on to the next, and to leave the cash drawer open only long enough to make change, the till tapper will not have an opportunity to steal.

CUSTOMER INJURY AND LAWSUITS

Some companies seem to almost ask for serious customer lawsuits. The loss here, of course, is obvious, both in lawyers' fees and in unfavorable judgments.

It is suggested that management assign an alert, imaginative employee to report on conditions likely to cause serious injury to a customer or outsider. If one of the officials already has responsibility for employee safety, he or she can also handle this function. But this should never be a routine, checkoff-list type of assignment. A profit drain resulting from customer injury may seem like only a remote possibility, but a single incident can be very costly.

The employee responsible for safety should be completely objective in reporting dangerous conditions. The person should ask, "If existing conditions should deteriorate slightly, could a customer or passerby be injured or killed?"

Before a policy is set for dealing with customer injury claims, it should be reviewed by the company lawyer. Then the policy should be made known to employees so they can protect the company's interests and promptly advise management of all claims or injuries. Depending on the legal advice received, management may want to immediately interview witnesses and obtain signed statements when an incident of this kind occurs.

Almost any business may have some potential vulnerability to customer injury. A customer may trip over merchandise in the aisles of a retail store. Even a small business may use some acids or corrosive chemicals that may be available to children playing in the alleyway behind the establishment. If carbon dioxide is used to put out fires in the computer room, there is an outside possibility that a visitor might rush into the area with a hand extinguisher, only to be asphyxiated by the carbon dioxide. There are, of course, many other situations that depend on local conditions. Each company must examine its particular vulnerabilities.

CONCLUSION

Total security is unobtainable. For some areas, such as in the computer installation, there should be no compromise; for others, the objective should be to reduce the probability of loss to an acceptable level, at lowered cost.

Management must decide what is to be protected, and at what

hazards. Management must also decide what risks are worth taking when the likelihood of harm is extremely low, or when the cost of protection appears to be excessive.

Programs to lessen the impact of business crime must compete with other management projects for the allocation of operating dollars. This fact must be taken into account in planning and implementing controls.

Increasingly, management has turned away from the old ideas of security to the more effective approach of loss prevention. This is because no company can afford to have assets dissipated by poor product control, waste, pilferage, or internal theft. In many instances it may be as difficult to hold onto earnings as to make them in the first place. Profit percentages in many businesses are at an all-time low, and there simply may be nothing left if controls over business processes are ignored. In the past management has often failed to realize that many of these losses are avoidable. Preventive security as such is not a separate and distinct responsibility of management. It is so closely aligned with good management practices as to be inseparably linked with overall management competency.

APPENDIX

A workable set of company security rules

THE XYZ COMPANY has rules of conduct that must be observed by all employees. To do our job it is important to work together, and these rules have been drawn up to protect the rights and interests of everyone.

Neglect of responsibility and noncompliance with the rules of good conduct will not be allowed. This would be unfair to the remainder of the employees. When violations occur, it may be necessary for violators to be reprimanded, suspended without pay, or discharged from the job.

Serious action against an employee is never welcomed by the company, since we are interested in you as a person and want you to remain on the job with us. Then, too, we have an investment in you, since it is always expensive to recruit, hire, and train a replacement. And we may be unable to locate someone with your distinctive skills.

Let's consider some of the rules that must be observed in the best interests of everyone. This list is not complete, of course, but it does point out the practices that must be avoided.

The following are prohibited activities:

Possession or use of dangerous drugs, narcotics, or alcoholic beverages on the premises or parking lot. Also, reporting to work under the influence of drugs or alcohol.

Theft or removal of any company property from the premises, without proper authorization.

Fighting on company property, or during working hours.

Gambling on engaging in a lottery, including the sale of lottery tickets.

Engaging in any kind of sexual misconduct on company time, either on or off the premises, or soliciting another to become involved in such misconduct.

Falsifying personnel records or production figures.

Punching the time card of a fellow worker, having someone else punch the time card of the employee, or making unauthorized alterations on a payroll or time card record.

Removing or posting signs or other matter on company bulletin boards or company property at any time, unless approved in advance by management.

Swearing, making vicious, malicious, or profane statements concerning any supervisor, fellow worker, employee, the company, or its products.

Deliberately misusing, damaging, or destroying company property or the property of a co-worker.

Sleeping on the job, or hiding from a supervisor.

Deliberately restricting production or work.

Intimidating, threatening, coercing, or interfering with the activities of other employees on the premises.

Selling merchandise to other employees as a sideline, soliciting contributions for any purpose on company property, unless approved by management.

Participating in games, scuffling, horseplay, unnecessary shouting, or creating deliberate confusion on the premises.

Refusing to wear required safety clothing or equipment. Creating poor housekeeping conditions that compromise safety or sanitary conditions on company property. Performing assigned duties in a manner that threatens the safety of the employee or fellow workers.

Smoking in areas where such activity is prohibited.

Deliberately loitering, killing time, or leaving an assigned work position without authority or adequate reason.

Index